INVINCIBLE SUCCESS

**SELL WITH CONFIDENCE,
LEAD WITH PURPOSE,
AND SPEAK WITH IMPACT!**

MARK STEEL

WHAT PEOPLE ARE SAYING

"A brilliant blend of storytelling, useful insights, and a continuous focus on helping others succeed."
Curt Mercadante, Founder - Merc Enterprises, LLC and best-selling author of *Five Pillars of the Freedom Lifestyle*

"If you want to achieve the seemingly impossible, you must read *Invincible Success!*"
Vincent C Racioppo, PhD, President - Center for Expert Performance, Inc.

"*Invincible Success* is a must-read. It is a 'Must Have' toolkit for anyone in sales and leadership!"
Sherlaender "Lani" Phillips, Vice President of US Partner Sales - Microsoft

"If you want to fulfill your potential as a professional in sales, influence, and leadership then this is a must-read book. This is a powerful tool that I wish I would have had years ago."
Mareo McCracken, Chief Revenue Officer – Movemedical

"Imagine immediately improving your leadership, sales, and speaking; it is possible with *Invincible Success!* Mark's personal stories and practical ideas will be a game-changer for you!"
Sarah Victory, international speaker and bestselling author of *How to be Powerful*

"If you are looking to build your own business to stratospheric success, Mark's book is the place to start."
 Barbara Wichman, global speaker, leadership coach, and acclaimed author of *The Leadership Tinderbox*

"This book is a must-read for anyone who wants to positively impact and influence others. Mark Steel not only equips you with the bulletproof, superhero confidence that you need, he then teaches you how to use that confidence to powerfully and effectively connect and inspire others."
 Michelle Calloway, CEO - REVEALiO, Inc., Founder - Tech With Heart Foundation

"This book is a must-have for everyone."
 Tanjia M. Coleman, PhD

"Full of essential techniques you can implement immediately!"
 Debbie Vyskocil, President - Optimal Edge Performance

"This is a fantastic read."
 Jake Jordan, Founder - Impact Over Attention

"It has instantly become part of our training."
 Cory Warfield, Co-Founder and Chief Visionary Officer – Shedwool

This book is packed with action steps that anyone in sales, leadership, or speaking can put to use immediately. Mark's storytelling makes this book compelling, clear, and inspiring. Do yourself a favor, get this book today. Highly recommend!
 Shay Rowbottom, CEO - Shay Rowbottom Marketing

Invincible Success

Copyright © 2020 by Mark Steel

RHG Media Productions
25495 Southwick Drive #103
Hayward, CA 94544.

All rights reserved. No part of this publication may be reproduced distributed or transmitted in any form or by any means including photocopying recording or other electronic or mechanical means without proper written permission of author or publisher, except in the case of brief quotations embodied in critical reviews and certain other noncommercial uses permitted by copyright law.

ISBN 9781735463308 (paperback)
ISBN 9781735463315 (hardcover)

Visit us on line at www.YourPurposeDrivenPractice.com

Printed in the United States of America.

For Jodi, my love.
and
For those of you who find fulfillment in serving others.

CONTENTS

WHAT PEOPLE ARE SAYING 3
CONTENTS 9
ACKNOWLEDGEMENTS 11
INTRODUCTION 13
ARE YOU READY TO BE INVINCIBLE? 17
    Understanding Invincible 18
    Making Invincible Personal 21
    Knowing Invincible Is Possible 23
UNLOCKING RELENTLESS DETERMINATION 27
    The External Challenge 29
    It Only Takes A Spark 33
    Two Powerful Strategies:
        Networking and Learning 35
YOU ARE NOT AN IMPOSTOR 41
    Understanding Impostor Syndrome 45
    Overcoming the Internal Challenge 48
    The Danger of Complacency 51
INVINCIBLE PRINCIPLE 1: CREATE INTENTIONAL CONNECTION 55
    Learning to Listen As You Listen to Learn 57
    How to Ask 60
    Become a Master Discoverer 63
INVINCIBLE PRINCIPLE 2: BUILD LASTING TRUST 69
    Your Ability Is Your Credibility 71
    Consistency Is Key 74
    Have Integrity in All That You Do 78
    You Are Responsible 81
INVINCIBLE PRINCIPLE 3: DEFINE A BOLD VISION 87
    See What They Do Not See 89
    Differentiate Through Value 93
    The Strength of Your Team 97

INVINCIBLE PRINCIPLE 4: SPEAK WITH IMPACT 101
    A Strong Opening 104
    A Clear Solution 108
    The Compelling Close 112

INVINCIBLE PRINCIPLE 5: SHARE GREAT STORIES 117
    Discovering Stories Around You 120
    Developing Your Stories 123
    The Magic is in Your Delivery 127

INVINCIBLE PRINCIPLE 6: FOSTER LASTING BELIEF 133
    Achieving Big Growth 135
    Celebrate With Gratitude 140
    Believing Is Seeing 143

YOU ARE INVINCIBLE 149
ABOUT THE AUTHOR 155
IN GRATITUDE 157
REVIEWS 159

ACKNOWLEDGEMENTS

I would like to thank the talented and insightful Sarah Victory for being the spark that made this book possible. Sarah and I first met over a stack of pancakes. During our breakfast, she looked at me and said, "You have a message inside you that was meant to be heard." A little more than a year later, here it is. To Sarah, I am eternally grateful.

I am thankful for Suzanne Nance, who is not only the first American woman to accomplish the Explorer's Grand Slam but also one heck of a coach. Thank you for stepping in at the last minute to save me from the crevasse of vocabulary repetition.

Thank you to Rebecca Hall Gruyter and her team at RHG for helping bring this book to life. Your partnership and patience were greatly appreciated.

Many thanks go to all who contributed to the impactful stories you find inside. This includes those specifically cited in the text as well as others who also spoke with me such as Jeff Markowitz, Deepak Rao, Jeff Gettis, Bill Topel, Greg Widerski, Adam Burke, Tom Mesi, Michael Cole, David Roeser, Bob Roudebush, Jean-Marc Krikorian, Chris Sellers, Dan Hoppe, Kelly Carlson, Naresh Koka, Doug Fulton, Irina Ioffe, Tony Jalen, Joel Fitzpatrick, JP Morgenthal, Douglas Ennis, Greg Laos, Gauri Chawla, Natalija Paldrmich, John McCahan, Chris Torrence, Ahmed Hedayat, and Gary Siegel. While I ran out of pages to include everyone, the culmination of your experiences and insights contributed to the overall quality of content here.

My deepest gratitude goes to the many mentors, peers, and friends who have supported me in my career. Those wonderful people include Adam Hecktman, Alisa Swann, Lani Phillips,

Jesse Washington, Mark Litwin, Nancy Depcik, Debbie Vyskocil, Conor Cunneen, the late Ret. Col. Jill Morgenthaler, Stella Lorens, Christian Banach, Jim McNeeley, Jake Jordan, Dutch McAllyster, and many more.

Thank you, Mom, for your love, Rod for being the role model of putting your all into everything you do, and Matt for your endless support while showing me the places I will go.

Finally, thank you to my amazing wife, Jodi, who served as lead editor and Encourager-in-Chief. Your love fills me up every day. Also, thank you to my wonderful children, Jace and Cassidy. I am proud to be your Dad.

INTRODUCTION

"Begin with the end in mind."
—Steven Covey

You have a gift.

Your gift may be a product or service. It may be an idea. It may be knowledge, experience, or vision. It may be your creativity, state of mind, or ability to execute. Your gift may be a combination of all these things.

Your gift is unique. It is transformative. It can enhance the lives of individuals, enterprises, and communities. It can change the way we come together, collaborate, and accomplish greatness.

The world needs your gift.

The challenge is, your special gift only helps others when shared in such a way that others want to spend their all-too-precious time, energy, or money on it.

You have an opportunity to communicate your gift in a way that compels people to invest in it. This book will ensure you embrace that opportunity in a powerful way.

If your goal is to Sell with Confidence, Lead with Purpose, or Speak with Impact, this book is for you. It contains steps that you can quickly take to enhance your career and personal life significantly. The principles outlined here will result in building deeper connections with those you serve and inspiring them to take action. You will also find useful strategies that will enable you to respond to challenges on the path to extraordinary accomplishments. Though this book is primarily intended for those focused on improving sales and leadership skills, anyone with lofty goals and a passion to succeed can use the easy-to-implement, repeatable methodology outlined here to make that happen. If you are already a sales superhero or in your first sales role, an established leader or climbing up the career ladder, a recognized expert or just getting started, this book will amplify your results while energizing your career. Whether you are looking to triumph at home or work, or you are looking to change the world, make it happen by learning to thrive!

Invincible Success is a culmination of powerful strategies acquired from years of experience and research. In this book, I share the methods and insights that took me from my first sales job, where I felt like a fraud and almost got fired, to thriving as a sales leader while contributing to over $1 billion in sales. In addition, you will hear from dozens of executives and global sales leaders who were interviewed for the book. They share insights and stories of overcoming profound challenges to achieve their own Invincible Success. The collective years of industry knowledge and hands-on experience will eliminate countless setbacks and moments of frustration in your quest to achieve the outcomes you seek.

By following the principles laid out in this book, you WILL empower yourself and others, you WILL be more confident and engaging, and you WILL achieve extraordinary results.

The essence of sales, leadership, and effective communication is largely the same. Start with a compelling offering, find the people who can benefit from that offer, then tell them about your offering in a way that moves them to take action. That seems simple enough. However, let's be straight with each other. Though the goal may be simple, you still have work to do. Your offerings—your unique products, ideas, abilities, or perspectives—are indeed amazing, yet there are many other people out in the marketplace who have their own unique products, ideas, abilities, and perspectives. Because of that, your potential customers, team members, and audiences are inundated with ads, emails, and an ever-growing number of other priorities. There are endless distractions vying for your customers' time and attention. As more businesses enter the marketplace, it becomes harder to differentiate yourself. This continuous change and challenge are the reality of doing business today.

Then there is the *unexpected*. As I write this in the spring of 2020, the world is facing a crisis of historic proportions. A pandemic is sweeping across the globe, affecting every person and every business on the planet. The loss of life is devastating. Unemployment is skyrocketing. The uncertainty and apprehension in the marketplace are palpable. Organizations are scrambling to survive. The toll on businesses and the global economy is profound. Though the situation continues to evolve, it is already clear that most businesses and industries will be changed forever.

It is a sobering reality. However, it is not the whole reality. There is more to this moment than grief and confusion. Every day, heroes are responding to the crisis. People are connecting, sharing ideas, and finding new ways to work together. Businesses are already adapting to their circumstances. As that happens, it creates new scenarios for you to assist them. Even as customers scramble to redefine the way they do business, there are opportunities for you to make certain they thrive.

Whether you are reading this book while the world still grapples with a health and economic crisis, or whether you are reading this book far in the future, there is an opportunity to ensure your customer's success. No matter whether the economic situation in this moment is causing a slowdown in spending or the economy is growing at a rapid pace, the following statement will still be true: **The people you serve need you now more than ever before.**

In the first chapter, together, we will define what it means to be Invincible. You will set yourself up to get the most out of this book by understanding just what Invincible means to you. Next, we will learn powerful strategies to take on the challenges you will face in creating a career that inspires you every day. Then we dive into the proven process for sales, leadership, and speaking success. I first developed this process in my high-impact sales career and now share it with sales teams and leaders in global organizations. The closing chapters reveal the key ingredient that will wrap itself around everything we covered, amplifying your results. Along the way, there are tips to serve as reminders and "Success Step" exercises to reinforce key learnings.

Before we begin, there is one note on terminology used in the book. You will notice I frequently refer to "your customer" as those people who are central to your application of the processes in this book. Some of you may take issue with the term and think, "I'm not in sales. I don't have customers." Do not let the term "customer" throw you. Regardless of your career or personal goals, the term "customer" simply refers to the person or people you serve or are hoping to impact. In that way, "customer" could easily be replaced with: client, direct report, audience, attendee, executive committee, donor, volunteer, and many more.

In sales, the use of the term "customer" is obvious. But there are times when salespeople need to apply the same "customer" principles to interactions involving managers, peers, and partners. For leaders, your "customers" may be your management team, your board of directors, or team members, or employees. As a speaker, your "customers" are those people to whom you are speaking as you strive to educate and inspire. We all have customers. Yet, for relatability, I encourage you to substitute the appropriate word that best fits the group of individuals you interact with most often.

It is time to move forward! As you do, know that there is no limit to what is possible. Define what outcomes you wish to achieve and then make them happen. Unleash creativity and vision. Build stronger relationships. See opportunities to transform. Feel ambitious and energized. Gain confidence. Motivate your team. Adapt to change. Outsmart your competition. You can have it all! **All you need is the spark to ensure you reach your peak potential.**

Let this book be that spark. This is the moment to transform. It is time to become unflappable, unshakeable, and unstoppable. **It is time to become Invincible!**

Mark Steel
Sales & Leadership Keynote Speaker & Consultant
https://marksteel.com

ARE YOU READY TO BE INVINCIBLE?

"You can always amend a big plan, but you can never expand a little one. I don't believe in little plans."
—Harry S. Truman

When was the last time you believed you were Invincible?

Think back to when you were a kid. Did you ever pretend to have special powers? Most kids, girls and boys alike, dream of having some type of magical power. Do you remember? Were you Unstoppable or Incredible or Super?

When I was a boy, I fully believed I was Invincible. I proclaimed it to my mom and dad, my brothers, and that happy little boy who always seemed to hang out in the hallway mirror. Of course, back then, to be Invincible, all I needed was a towel for a cape, a t-shirt, and some superhero underwear. I would run around the house, climbing on chairs, the arms of couches, and when Mom was not looking, the dining room table. Every time I climbed up on something, I would declare to the world:

"I AM INVINCIBLE!"

What was your powerful belief?

Unfortunately, as we get older, that belief fades away. We either tell ourselves or are told by others that such thoughts are not real. After all, ordinary people do not have superpowers, right? As time goes on, we start to limit ourselves. We choose to fit in rather than stand out. Where we once thought we could not be stopped, by the time we are adults, we are holding ourselves back from the incredible career and life success we deserve. It does not have to be this way.

What would it take for you to believe you were Invincible again?

That is exactly what this book is going to do — This book will make you INVINCIBLE!!

That may seem like a bold, audacious claim. It is. This daring claim is one that I have the fullest confidence you can achieve. Much of that claim is because of the fact that I *believe in you*. I believe that you are overwhelmingly capable of incredible things. I believe you can build a highly successful and fulfilling career. You can serve others in a way that helps their business grow and their employees more productive. You can overcome indecision and doubts about your own abilities by consistently exceeding the goals you create. When that happens, you feel more empowered and confident, propelling you into even more extraordinary results. Renowned psychologist Albert Bandura once said, "People's beliefs about their abilities has a profound effect on those abilities." In other words, **when you believe you are Invincible, you are.**

Here are the three key items important to reaching success:

1. Understanding Invincible
2. Making Invincible Personal
3. Knowing Invincible Is Possible

Understanding Invincible

To help you understand fully what being Invincible will mean for you, I will start by sharing what it means to me. It was not until a few years ago that I remembered that Invincible feeling I had as a little boy. I was struck by the wonderful memory. As I stood thinking about that special memory, I noticed something unexpected. I found myself feeling that same powerful, full-of-possibilities feeling that I had back then. I raised my arms in the victory pose, just as I did as a child. The energy I felt was exhilarating.

This got my attention, so I started layering the word "Invincible" into my keynote speeches and sales consultancy programs. Audiences and clients seemed to resonate instantly with the word and wanted to be Invincible themselves. Raising their arms in the air and shouting in unison soon became one of the highlights of my programs. Imagine how uplifting and fun it is to be in a room full of executives and sales leaders on their feet with their arms in the air shouting, "**I AM INVINCIBLE**!"

Yet, inevitably, a well-intentioned attendee would approach me after a speech and say, "I loved it! I loved everything you shared…" Then her voice would trail off. My eyes would narrow as I could feel the "but" coming. She continues, "But maybe you shouldn't say '*Invincible*.' People can't really be Invincible, right?" Some folks were even kind enough to rattle off examples of ways in which we are not Invincible. They point out that "bullets won't bounce off your chest" or "a meteor falling on your head would still hurt." Imagine my polite smile as I listen to a list of possible calamities.

Given that these days, Marvel and DC Comics movies are releasing at a near-continuous pace, I understood their response. For you, at first, the word Invincible might conjure up images of shapely superheroes making witty comments while they easily conquer their enemies. Because of that, right now I expect you to stand majestically at the top of a mountain in a spandex costume. While I do encourage anyone who wants to climb to the top of a mountain to do so, a Netflix-inspired version of Invincible is not what I mean.

Instead, imagine an instance when you felt strong even in the face of uncertainty. Maybe your team members were stressed about a deadline or customer situation, but you were confident the team would come through. If nothing comes to mind at work, is there an example from your personal life when there were challenges or moments of chaos, but you did not back away? Have you shown strength and resolve in the face of difficulty? I suspect you have.

It is that strength, that resolve, that clarity of purpose that we are striving for here. Habitually training yourself to work through challenge, change, and distraction. It is a mindset of always moving forward, growing through learning and failure. Knowing what you have, how you are going to move forward, and then refusing to quit. When working with sales teams, leaders, and speakers, my simple definition is:

When you combine a unique offering with relentless determination and a proven process to achieve results, you are Invincible.

As we move through this book, we will examine two of these components in detail. The one area we will not specifically cover is your unique offering. As mentioned in the introduction, your unique offering may vary depending on your role and current goal. Most often, this is a physical product or well-defined service offering. However, your unique offering may also be your ideas, insights, abilities, inspiration, or other less tangible offerings. For the most part, I am going to assume you know what that unique offering is. If you are still trying to define what your offering is, there are plenty of books and podcasts out there to help.

One note of clarification is that, in truth, *you* are your unique offering. You may have a physical product that you sell or a service that you provide, but unless you are doing internet commerce, your customers are buying *you*. This is true in sales and when speaking in front of others. It is especially true for leaders. Who you are, what you stand for, and how you make others feel contributes to what you offer to others. As this book will make you more confident, connected to others, and impactful, it will be developing the product of you. That is a happy side effect rather than a focus of *Invincible Success*.

Consider my definition of what it means to be Invincible only as helpful context. It is meant to get you thinking of what is possible. However, before we lay out the proven process and relentless determination to achieve that you will use to become Invincible, we must make the definition of Invincible more personal to you. It is only through that personalization and commitment that we get a full awareness of where we are going.

MAKING INVINCIBLE PERSONAL

To define what Invincible means to you, I encourage you to take an assessment of where you are today in your quest to achieve success. To do that, I developed a simple tool that you can use to determine how ready you are to be Invincible. You can quickly access this free tool at invinciblesuccess.com/index. This Invincibility Index tool will ask you a series of questions that you will use to determine your score. I encourage you to write down the score and keep it in a place you will be able to find later. In doing so, you can track your progress throughout your development and growth.

I created the Invincibility Index tool over time as I worked with clients. As we worked together, I found that by having them answer a few questions, we were able to track progress in our sessions together. Some of my more competitive clients enjoyed pushing themselves to raise their score over time. More importantly, the Invincibility Index tool is intended to get you thinking of the various areas of growth we will be focusing on in this book.

Once you have used the Invincibility Index to understand where you stand today, it is time to define what Invincible means to you. This is important to determine so that you know exactly where to focus your energy going forward. The definition of Invincible will be different for everyone. To personalize the strategies and steps in this book, take a moment to answer the question, **"What would I do if I were Invincible?"**

Keep your exploration focused on your career for now. What does success mean to you? What would you be doing in your career? What would you change about your job? Is there a different role or industry in which you would be working? Do you strive to be one of the highest achievers, reaching the President's Club by adding more to the business than any of your peers? Would it mean you are pushing outside your comfort zones, going after the roles that would challenge you to grow?

Perhaps you want to be a recognized thought-leader. Are you planning to be a top executive or a high-performing individual contributor? Have you have always wanted to start a business? Do you imagine sharing a message that is heard by hundreds, thousands, or millions of people? Keep in mind, as you explore, you do not need to know how to make it happen. The 'How' does not matter in this moment. We are only concerned about defining 'What' Invincible means in your career and personal life.

 **Success Step**

Write down 3 examples of what your career and life would look like if you were Invincible. In other words, define what success means to you. Be as specific as possible. Use this chance to dare greatly. After all, you are Invincible. If you could do anything you choose, what would that be? Who would you impact? In what way would you impact them? Knowing where you are going will ensure you stay on track.

As you reach new levels of achievement, you still have the freedom to make changes to any Invincible goals. Your definition of what success means to you may change throughout your career. This change can be planned or may come from unforeseen situations. In 2014, when an unexpected tragedy took her husband from her, Jody LaVoie was suddenly thrust into leading the multimillion-dollar organization he had founded years earlier. In that moment, success was being able to lean on her amazing team of employees to help her navigate the business through the difficult time. After she led the company to significant growth, it was later acquired. Jody then went on to become CEO of Female Strong, an organization dedicated to empowering female leaders and entrepreneurs. Throughout this journey, Jody's goals shifted as new opportunities came her way. You have the same leeway in your own journey.

Did you write down three examples of what Invincible means to you? If not, please do so. Keep that paper or electronic copy handy.

I encourage you to look back at it at the beginning of each month. Determine whether you are closer to one of those 3 examples of success that you wrote down or if any adjustments are needed. By defining what Invincible Success means to you and routinely tracking your progress, you build confidence and create marvelous momentum.

Knowing Invincible Is Possible

Understanding what it means to be Invincible and then personalizing it leads us to the final important component needed for this book to work. **Believe that you *can* be Invincible—because you can.** You can refine goals, learn processes, and develop the mindset to be an Invincible salesperson, leader, or speaker.

Remember, when you combine a unique offering with relentless determination and a proven process to achieve results, you are Invincible. This means that you do not need to outwork everyone around you while only sleeping 3 hours a day. Does it demand a great deal of effort? Yes. But would you want it any other way? If exceptional results were easier, everyone around you would be achieving them, too. This would mean your work would never stand out. Accomplishing big things takes work. Laziness is easy; success takes effort. Leave the laziness for those who accept mediocrity.

Will there be challenges? Of course. The next two chapters will equip you to handle those challenges. When you are creative, agile, and able to handle what comes your way, you will easily deal with these challenges as they arise. A customer tells you they do not have the budget. No problem. You lean in and help them find even more value in their investment. Your team is feeling anxious about reaching this year's quota? You rally them together in a way that enables them to deliver. You have a critical speech coming up for investors that will make or break your startup? Not only do you get the funding you need, but your speech also generates such interest that you exceed your highest funding goals. Small or large business, teams of 1 or 1000, whether you are talking to your first customer or have been at this for years, you are Invincible.

Even better, you already have everything that you need. You are carrying it inside of you. Today, at this very moment, you have what it takes. The resources are within you. It is time to tap into those resources and build a repeatable system that ensures you can handle whatever comes at you. Believing you can achieve Invincible results will open those powerful parts of you in an intentional and consistent way. Regardless of where you find yourself today, you can create even bigger results. You can upgrade your career, financial status, relationships, health, and your impact on the world. **Invincible is possible!**

Invincible Tips

1. Determine your Invincibility Index Score
2. Open yourself up to becoming Invincible
3. Write down what Invincible means to you
4. Let yourself believe that Invincible is possible

Summary

You have a product or service that you want to share with others. That is all you need to start off your journey to becoming Invincible. The next step is to personalize what exactly Invincible means to you. What will you do differently 6 months, 12 months, or 2 years from now because you have created an Invincible mindset? What will your customers and team members be saying about the Invincible you? By personalizing your Invincible goals, you now have a solid foundation on which to layer the determination and proven process to reach success. There is still work needed to get through the journey; however, it is worth the effort. In fact, the reward for doing the work necessary to build the career and life you seek will pale in comparison to the happiness you get from knowing you didn't stop until you accomplished things most people only dream of. Even better, soon you will learn to love the journey you are on. You will marvel at how much higher you can go.

When you are Invincible, Success is Inevitable.

UNLOCKING RELENTLESS DETERMINATION

"When you accept yourself with your worthiness and weakness, you are invincible."
— Dr Anil Kr Sinha

Years ago, I was captivated by the opening to *Mission: Impossible 2*. There was something about it that stuck with me. The movie opens with the main character, Ethan Hunt, played by actor Tom Cruise, out for a leisurely climb up the side of a massive rock tower in the Utah desert. Not only is he 2,000 feet in the air, but we see he has no safety rope. Despite the danger, Ethan is firmly in control. His cool control is further highlighted when he hurls himself into the air, leaping from one stone pillar to another and perfectly sticking the landing.

Yet suddenly, Ethan loses his footing and is instantly sliding down a slippery rock ledge. He frantically grabs for something to save him before plunging over the edge and beginning to fall. However, in one last agonizing attempt to live, his hand catches the tiniest of stone outcroppings and he stops himself from falling. My entire body clenched as I saw Ethan dangling 2,000 feet in the air, precariously holding on by his fingertips.

Now, years after watching the movie, it is that image and that frightened, desperate feeling that comes to mind when I look back on those moments in my life when I felt an utter lack of control. Two of these "fingertip moments," these moments of desperation and fear, have had a profound effect on both my career and personal life. They have also been two of the most insightful and transformative times in my life. Before I share with you the first of these two moments, it is important to understand what can cause a "fingertip moment" and how to arm yourself with strategies to prevent them.

To reach the success we want to reach, we must have relentless determination. This takes ongoing effort. To reach our sales goals or become respected leaders and speakers takes a level of perseverance that very few possess. Create the determination needed to reach any goal by developing habits that will grow both energy and fulfillment.

As noted, you will run into challenges, both large and small, as you work toward the goals defined in the last chapter. Small challenges, such as being stopped by a gatekeeper when trying to reach a decision-maker or a member of your team consistently not pulling his or her weight. You may face large challenges, such as dealing with the fallout from a product recall or a seed investor pulling out of your startup. These types of challenges could make you feel like you are sliding out of control.

Most challenges we face in our careers (and lives) are isolated and can be dealt with as they arise. However, at times, we may be hit with many cascading setbacks that seem to arise in rapid succession, or we are hit with an obstacle so significant we may have limited capacity to respond. If these challenges are unable to be resolved quickly, we may start to feel tremendous anxiety and a loss of control. If these feelings continue, we may reach a "fingertip moment" of extreme desperation. We reduce the chances of this happening when we identify the problem quickly and respond accordingly.

Obstacles can come from either external or internal forces. **An external challenge comes from someone or something other than yourself.** A struggling global economy or a world health crisis are two examples of external challenges that the world is facing today, as are unexpected job loss, customer funding issues, or any number of things that happen without your direct influence.

On the other hand, **internal challenges can include self-doubt, lack of motivation, or poor planning**. An internal issue could also come from insufficient knowledge on a particular subject, inconsistent work on your behalf, or a lack of focus or organization. Internal challenges come from within your sphere of influence.

As you encounter these obstacles, take a moment to identify whether it is external or internal. Essentially, is this problem being caused by someone or something other than you, or is it being caused by something *you* are or are not doing? By identifying whether the issue is outside, inside, or both, you can respond with the appropriate techniques. Using this analysis, you will know how best to respond. We will start by examining strategies to deal with external challenges before moving on to internal challenges in the next chapter.

The External Challenge

Do not be fooled by the idea of an outside problem being something over which you have no control. Yes, at the outset, by its very nature, an external challenge is caused by someone or something other than you. But it is still a challenge happening to you. You still need to be able to respond and handle these outside forces in an effort for you to reach your goals.

One external challenge in sales and leadership positions is frequent job changes. Studies show that sales jobs are notoriously high in turnover. One study, conducted by Bridge Group in 2015, **found a 34% attrition rate for sales positions**. This means that even if your job has not been taken away unexpectedly, you very likely will be going through multiple job changes in your career.

Add to that, most organizations today are under continuous pressure to increase innovation, produce more with less, and out-maneuver their competition. Companies must evolve or die. Since one of the most flexible assets of a company is its people, that means the employees often bear the brunt of this pressure. You may find your job description is being rewritten each year. Often, every few months. **As this trend continues, are you prepared?**

Years ago, an unexpected new role with a significantly different job description led to the biggest external challenge I have ever faced in my career. It was the first time in my working life that I felt like I was in a situation far over my head with no idea how I was going to get out. Today, I look back with pride at my 15-year sales career at Microsoft, but back then, my career nearly ended shortly after it began.

In the late 90s, I moved to Chicago to pursue an acting career. To pay the bills and put food on the table, I signed with a temporary placement agency to get day work. Fairly quickly, I was placed in a long-term administrative job at the local Microsoft sales office. At the time, I did not know much about Microsoft or their technology, but the full-time employment during the day allowed me to do theatre at night.

Imagine my shock when, after eighteen months of this "temporary assignment," a sales manager named Adam Hecktman approached me and offered me a job as a Technical Evangelist on a brand-new team. Joining his team would be far different from anything I had done before. In fact, prior to that job offer, I had no previous technology or sales experience. I was shocked he was taking such a chance on me. It wasn't until many years later that Adam told me, "Every day I saw you working hard as a temp. Then, during your downtime, I'd spot you reading books on Microsoft technology. Your job was to answer the phones and here you were trying to learn Windows 98. I didn't think I was taking a chance at all."

This new job at Microsoft was outside of my comfort zone for sure. Fortunately, I was hired to take on a very specific role. With my public speaking background, my job was to deliver presentations to technology enthusiasts and folks working in the information technology field. Each day, I educated rooms full of people, getting them excited about upcoming product releases. When not presenting, I was constantly learning. I met with peers, watched hundreds of hours of training content, and did many months of late-night cram sessions on my own. By the end of my first year as an evangelist, I felt like all that extra hard work was paying off. I had a growing grasp of the products, the marketing team enjoyed working with me, and feedback from my presentations was highly rated. My misgivings were melting away, and I was feeling comfortable in my new career.

Can you predict what happened next? Toward the end of that first year, I was called into Adam's office. Since this was all new to me, I was not aware that in such a fast-paced industry, change is frequent. Adam said, "Mark, you really are doing a great job. Your feedback scores are high, and the team thinks the world of you. However, going into next year the evangelist role has been eliminated. Your job is now a sales specialist." As he saw the incredulous look on my face, he reassuringly added, "You're going to do great."

In a matter of moments, my job description had radically altered. I was no longer an evangelist giving presentations to tech enthusiasts. I was now a salesperson on the frontlines of the largest technology organization in the world. In a flash, my job had morphed into a role where I was to be the technical expert, routinely meeting with top-level executives and directors of information technology at Fortune 100 organizations. **Instantly, all the confidence I had been building was gone.** Have you ever had your career radically shifted like that? Perhaps as the result of an organizational realignment or merger, you were moved to another team with different responsibilities.

If the evangelist role had been outside my comfort zone, this new sales role was so different from my previous one that I could no longer even *see* my comfort zone. Nevertheless, I was determined to do a great job. I can still remember one of the very first customer presentations I was asked to deliver. This would be for the new Chief Information Officer (CIO) of a well-known financial services customer. As I prepared, I thought, "This is my chance to make a great impression with a new executive." My goal was to come across as knowledgeable and self-assured. As the meeting started, I said, "We really understand financial services. We know what your challenges are. Businesses like yours struggle with 'this' and have a hard time with 'that.' Our team is here to help." From there I smoothly transitioned into my sales pitch. I was not more than 10 minutes into the conversation when the CIO promptly stood up and barked, "This is a waste of my time!" As I stood there, unable to formulate a response, he turned and walked out of the room. How is that for a welcome to my new sales career?

For the rest of that year, I struggled to uncover any new leads. Nothing seemed to move my sales cycles forward. I started getting more and more desperate, frantically doing my best to figure out what I could do differently that would magically turn things around. However, nothing seemed to work. My struggles continued through the end of my first fiscal year in the sales role. **When the financial books closed for the fiscal year, I was at 57% of my quota.** In other words, I missed my sales target by a mile.

I was dejected. I felt like a complete failure. I thought, "I was right! I knew they were making a terrible mistake. I am not good at sales! How could I have thought I could succeed in sales with no previous experience?" I wanted to quit, to run away from this job that I was clearly no good at. If I didn't quit, I was convinced I was going to be fired. If the external pressure from my customers and the organization were not enough, by that time, my wife Jodi was pregnant. I felt scared and not in control. I needed to find something to turn things around, and I needed it *now*!

With my job on the line, I knew my time for trial and error was over. It was time for me to stop trying to figure out sales success all on my own. To produce different results, I needed to take different actions. To do that as quickly and effectively as possible, I had to learn from people who were already getting the results I desired. **I needed to find people that were already successful and replicate their formula.**

It Only Takes A Spark

It was time to learn from the best. Fortunately, there was one seller who had always stood out from the pack. His name was Michael. Michael was a sales legend. Not just in our area, but he was one of those sellers you knew they talked about back at headquarters. That is because **Michael was just one of those people who was so good, he made sales seem effortless.** Have you worked with people like this?

Because of his amazing reputation, I was nervous to approach Michael. One day, I saw him in the office and said, "I am really struggling. My sales numbers are terrible. I can't seem to get any momentum with my customers. I've tried as many sales strategies as I can find. What's your secret?" What he responded back to me completely changed the trajectory of my sales and leadership career.

With a slight smile, Michael said to me, "I don't have a secret. There is just something I remind myself before I walk into a customer meeting. Before any meeting, I remind myself I am there to serve my customer. I'm there to solve their challenges." And then he said something that still moves me today. He said, **"You want to be great at this? Stop trying to be great at *sales*. Instead, be great at serving your customer."**

Experienced salespeople may think that advice was obvious, but back then it was a new concept for me. I remember walking away not exactly sure I knew what the heck Michael was talking about. However, after that brief conversation, I felt a spark inside me. It was as if he had somehow turned me in the right direction and had given me a nudge. I was determined to turn things around by putting my customer first.

I started approaching each meeting with this new perspective, focused on becoming great at serving my customer. I realized that these meetings were not about me, my company, or my sales pitch. **My customer meetings should be about my customer and *their* issues.** Armed with this new thinking, I made it a point to start every meeting by asking questions. My goal became to learn as much about my customers as I could. I could not solve their challenges unless I knew what they were.

The results were almost instantaneous. My customers started sharing their needs. I listened intently and asked clarifying questions, which led them to share even more. Once I felt I fully knew their issues, only then would I start to offer ways we could improve on what processes or tools they had in place today. By ditching my canned sales pitches, the dynamics of my meetings changed dramatically. My customers thanked me for listening. They told me how productive they felt the meetings had become. **Learning about their problems at such a deep level started creating new opportunities.** Soon, my sales pipeline went from frightening to thriving.

I ended that second year at 108% of my sales quota. An unbelievable turnaround for me! Encouraged, I became determined to build a process I could use to grow and achieve results consistently. Since talking to Michael had been so beneficial to me, I pushed myself to keep learning from others. I asked my most successful peers to serve as mentors to me, amplifying my growth. Where I had previously resisted asking others for help, I challenged myself with monthly goals on how many peers with whom I could speak. I also started reading sales and leadership books from authors including Jeff Olson, Collins & Parros, Brian Tracy, Dale Carnegie, Stephen Covey, Napoleon Hill, and many more.

I set a goal of mastering all aspects of my customer and team interactions. In my role, I had a front-row seat to learn from some of the best salespeople, leaders, and speakers working at that time. I watched what they did well and where I felt they could have improved. From all this learning, I developed a repeatable methodology that I could consistently follow to ensure my greatest opportunity for success. This methodology enhanced my entire approach to serving my customers. **It also became the foundation for the proven process to achieve the results outlined in this book.**

Two Powerful Strategies: Networking and Learning

Without that spark from Michael, I am not sure how I would have saved my job. That brief conversation pushed me to think differently about my approach to serving my customers. Beyond that immediate benefit, I discovered the two powerful strategies that I now use to respond to almost any challenge that comes my way. Both strategies have also become a central part of my growth and goal planning. The two powerful techniques that reshaped my success—**Nurture Your Network and Lifelong Learning**.

When it came to Networking, I will admit, prior to my Microsoft career, this was not an area of strength for me. I had been told countless times that I should always be building my network. But I did not really understand why. After all, I seemed pretty good at getting and keeping jobs. Plus, I was convinced that I could earn my roles on the merits of my work, not based on who I knew. Besides, asking people for help is *hard*, right? What I did not realize back then is networking is not about your next job. It is not about how that other person can help you. **Growing your network is about improving the quality of your career (and life).**

Yes, it is that valuable. Setting aside all of the times I have been explicitly helped by some of the wonderful people in my network, which are many, I have lost count of the number of times a conversation with someone new led to them sharing something I was able to use to refine my methods or avoid potential challenges. Beyond that, I unexpectedly developed friendships that continue today, simply by growing my network.

Bestselling author and wildly successful TEDx speaker, Susan Cain, agrees. The co-founder of Quiet Revolutions writes that networking "enriches [her] life every day." In fact, she encourages us to not think of it as networking; instead, think of it simply as "finding your people." Are you finding your people? What conscious steps are you taking to connect with new people on a routine basis? Is there more you can be doing in this regard?

Few know the strength of nurturing your network more than Gary Frey. Today, Gary works to help CEOs and other top executives overcome the challenge of scaling, aligning, and executing in their business. We first met on LinkedIn, where I quickly came to see the value he provides to others. Wanting to know more about him, I asked Gary to be a guest on my *Invincible Success* podcast. During the interview, he shared with me the greatest external challenge he ever faced in his career and how he was able to have the determination to move forward.

Years ago, after Gary was unexpectedly betrayed by a former friend and business partner, he recovered quickly by taking a leadership role at another ad agency on the other side of the country. After moving his family across the country and bringing in a multi-million-dollar client from his old firm, Gary soon was executing on a plan that would generate tremendous growth. In less than six months, Gary found himself the victim of another shocking betrayal, this time by his partner at the new firm. One minute, Gary was feeling confident in his bright future; the very next minute, his career collapsed into nothingness.

Unemployed and unsure of how he was going to take care of his young family, one afternoon while watching his son's soccer match, Gary reluctantly admitted his situation to another father watching the game. Within a few weeks, that stranger had helped Gary find a new leadership role at the company where he worked. That new opportunity got Gary back on his feet, reestablished his career, and launched him into even higher levels of success.

Understanding the strength in his network, Gary was able to bounce back from two devastating career setbacks. Apply this to your own career. Is there someone in your network today or someone you have yet to meet who may someday uncover an opportunity for you? Are there people out there waiting to be lifted by the value you can provide?

Tim Esplin, the Regional VP of Sales at Coupa Software sees nurturing his network as a way to grow and strengthen himself.

Tim says, "I try to take something away from the conversation with anyone I meet." In my conversation with George Kahlife, the host of the "Let's Grab Coffee" podcast adds, "Networking is about value, not numbers. You can have 600,000 connections on LinkedIn, but none of them bring you value. Focus on the small number that are more likely to add value or benefit from your offering."

 **SUCCESS STEP**

Make nurturing your network a planned part of your success routine. Determine what types of events you will attend and how many per month (One to two events per month is a manageable number for most). When meeting someone for the first time, make it a goal to learn about him as a person, not what he can do for you. Another tip is to use LinkedIn in the same way. When first connecting, avoid immediately asking for 30-minute phone calls. This is insincere and comes across that you are playing a numbers game by sending many requests a day. Instead, be genuine and intentional in your connection requests.

The second powerful strategy that will prepare you to respond to external challenges is Lifelong Learning. Have you ever watched a surfer perfectly riding a wave? An experienced surfer makes it look simply artistic. Yet, at a fundamental level, surfing is a process of staying just ahead of the wave threatening to crash down on you. It is keeping the surfboard far enough ahead of the wave to not get consumed by it. Apply the process to your own role. Imagine yourself riding the waves of innovation, changing customer needs, and organizational requirements just like that surfer. You can develop a system in which you flow through the challenges you face with the confidence of knowing you have what it takes to stay ahead.

Developing a lifelong learning mentality is the key to staying ahead. As a salesperson, automation is improving the process of moving an opportunity from lead to closing. Because of that, it is imperative that you stand out beyond "knowing your numbers."

Assume your peers will know their numbers, too. How will you differentiate yourself? As a leader, many of the reporting and dashboarding tools you use today are doing the work for you. This gives you an incredible opportunity to stand out from others in the way that you contribute to your customer's and team's success. In this way, **staying ahead depends more on the value you bring to your team and its impact on the organization.** This marketplace dynamic creates a tremendous chance for you to shine.

In his wonderful book *Linchpin*, Seth Godin describes the struggle happening in businesses as they try to cope with today's ever-changing marketplace. Godin writes that the office worker of today is becoming the factory worker of yesterday. Organizations are streamlining operations. As cloud computing becomes even more pervasive and artificial intelligence works its way into the software tools that we use each day, this threatens to drive down the value of an average worker. This means that each of us face the challenge of separating ourselves from others based on the creativity of our actions, not just the sheer amount of our work. What are you doing today that is making you irreplaceable in your industry or organization?

Success Step

Set time on your calendar at least 3 days a week dedicated to learning something new. I suggest you vary the topics you are learning, including some subjects not directly in your industry or field. There are many free or low-cost ways to learn today, including blogs, online magazines, YouTube, and LinkedIn Learning. By blocking your calendar and holding yourself to this structured time, you will become the Lifelong Learner you need to be to accomplish to stay ahead.

This growth mindset does not take a great deal of additional energy. Instead, it is about how you best apply your existing energy. **Lifelong learning is not about working harder than everyone** around you. **It is a matter of working smarter by adding a focus on continuous learning.**

Together, the powerful strategies of Nurturing Your Network and Lifelong Learning will ensure you have unlimited resources upon which to draw when you run into obstacles. By staying ahead of change, you are prepared to handle future challenges and you will find new and interesting ways to differentiate yourself. All along, you are seeking out others who may help you succeed while adding more value to your career and your life!

Invincible Tips

1. Ask yourself, "Am I ready for the unexpected?"
2. When you run into external challenges, call on your professional network
3. Become a Lifelong Learner by building learning into your structured routine
4. Stop trying to be great at sales. Instead, **be great at serving your customer**

Summary

Chances are that everyone reading this has faced her or his own "fingertips" moments, those crises or situations where you felt like you were lost or stuck or not feeling in control. These moments can happen with no notice whatsoever. Our careers can take unexpected turns or world events can reshape the way we do business. Yet, **even in the face of those external challenges that happen outside of your control, you are still responsible for what happens next**. To mitigate future issues, there are things you can be doing today to prepare. Find a mentor, coworker, or someone in your network who has had success in the areas in which you seek to grow. Your journey to success can be greatly enhanced as you consistently leverage the knowledge and experience of others. At the same time, look for activities that allow you to strengthen and grow your professional network. Be willing to provide value to others with no expectation it will be returned. Finally, commit to continuous learning to stay ahead and stand out from others. **This gives you the foundation you will need to develop the determination needed for your success**.

YOU ARE NOT AN IMPOSTOR

"Never compare yourself to others. Only compare the person you are today to the person you were the day before."
— Unknown

In the previous chapter, we discussed in depth the strategies needed to prevent and respond to external challenges, those that come at us from forces outside of our direct influence. However, too often, it is not the external forces that cause many of the issues we may face on the road to Invincible. Our own internal dialogue frequently becomes the source of our struggle to gain momentum. Because of this, it is important that we also develop strategies to conquer the internal challenges that stop us from creating the determination needed to reach lofty goals.

On the path to Invincible Success, there will be moments of doubt in your capacity to reach beyond your current situation. Depending on what new career obstacle you may be facing, it is not uncommon to wonder, "Do I have what it takes? Can I measure up?" This sense of uncertainty can appear in anyone. Momentary flashes of doubt appear in our minds and often fade away without much notice. In those cases, there is little reason to be concerned. Keep your forward progress rolling by trusting in your decision-making skills and ignoring those errant flickers of hesitation.

When self-doubt becomes more persistent, it can be very limiting. When we continue to feel uncertainty in more and more situations, we start to question our abilities and see ourselves through an unrealistic and distorted lens. For example, an upcoming important customer meeting, new service offering, or looming deadline may make you feel ill-equipped to rise to the occasion. Other examples include being too hard on yourself when things do not go exactly as planned or becoming obsessed with perceived gaps in knowledge instead of having confidence in your strengths. The resulting internal dialog can be debilitating.

It is hard to deny the accomplishments of Facebook Chief Operating Officer Sheryl Sandberg. She is a bestselling author, speaker, philanthropist, and activist. Yet she has struggled with the same doubts and lack of confidence that many of us have felt. In her book, *Lean In*, Sandberg outlines her feelings of not being enough. She shares, "Every time I was called on in class, I was sure I was about to embarrass myself. Every time I took a test, I was sure it had gone badly. And every time I didn't embarrass myself—or even excelled—I believed I had fooled everyone yet again. One day soon, the jig would be up."

As I read her words, I was certain Sheryl was speaking directly to me. Her story described some of the very same feelings with which I struggled early in my corporate career. My internal challenges began in the first year in my role and continued to grow in frequency and intensity as my career progressed. This ongoing struggle with confidence ultimately led to my second and most terrifying "hanging by my fingertips" moment.

As mentioned earlier, without any formal sales or technology experience before my Microsoft role, I had been surprised to find myself in a technical sales job for a leading organization. As I spent more time in the sales role, this initial shock changed into a nagging sense of uncertainty. I found myself wondering if I was ever going to be smart enough to grasp the technology or sales processes at a deep level. As I got to know colleagues and learned their backgrounds, I became acutely aware that I was surrounded by very bright, talented people. As you may expect, most everyone I met had bachelor's or master's degrees, while here I was with a little less than two years of community college. As my self-doubt grew, this seemingly trivial fact became the source of embarrassment and shame.

Year after year, even as I reached higher levels of sales success, fears of not being good enough continued to haunt me. It was as if I was carrying around a mental bag of rocks (something my friend and speaker Michelle Kim would call a "rockpack"). I struggled to understand technical concepts that seemed to come easily to my peers. Being too self-conscious to ask for help, I instead spent many (many!) evenings poring over my computer until the wee hours of the morning as I attempted to learn enough to feel competent the next day.

To further compensate for my self-perceived lack of qualifications, I believed the only way I could ever equal my coworkers was if I said "Yes" to every extra task or stretch assignment that came my way. When the nickname "Mr. Dependable" started showing up in my yearly reviews, that only served to reinforce my belief that I needed to take on even more. This created a downward spiral of feeling constantly overwhelmed. Rock after rock went into the mental bag.

As I contributed to more wins, I downplayed my contributions. I deflected praise by quickly responding, "I could not have done this without your help." Recognition made me uncomfortable as I told myself the awards, accolades, and advancement I was getting were a result of generous managers or kind coworkers. Even praise that resonated when I received it would quickly fade away. The negative self-talk always returned.

This swirl of harmful inner dialog started spinning into all aspects of my life. I felt trapped in my situation, unable to change. I withdrew from friends, family, hobbies, and my community. I fought for direction, often turning this fight onto my family. As our teenage son naturally grew more independent, our clashes for control grew frequent. This alienated my wife and young daughter, who were caught in the middle, causing me to push them away in confusion and shame. I withdrew further, becoming more isolated. These selfish acts of sabotage threatened to destroy everything important to me. I was alone, trapped, and felt I was just hanging by my fingertips.

In early 2013, at my lowest point, I stumbled across an internet article that changed the course of my life. The article discussed a psychological phenomenon known as Impostor Syndrome. I finally had a name for the inner turmoil and self-doubt that had plagued me for years. Even more encouraging, I learned I was far from alone. Finding so many others, just like me, thriving their way through this same level of doubt, gave me a glorious sense of relief. Those mental rocks, which had weighed me down for years, started falling from my pack.

Do my struggles sound like what you have felt in your career? If it does, know that you are not alone. Very successful individuals from many different industries and backgrounds have admitted to dealing with the internal challenges brought on by Impostor Syndrome. Beyond "famous people," you likely have friends, family, and peers who have had these same thoughts. People you know and leaders you admire may have had these thoughts.

I was reminded of this fact when I spoke to Sherlaender "Lani" Phillips, Vice President—US Channel Sales at Microsoft. Lani and I first met when she led the Midwest sales district, inclusive of the team I was on. Since then, she has been a leader and mentor to me, which has both inspired me and pushed me to grow. During a recent conversation, I asked Lani to tell me about one of the biggest challenges she has overcome in her impressive leadership career. After a brief pause, Lani confided, "Confidence." Her honesty is an example for us all.

Whether you feel you have Impostor Syndrome or not, you may recognize some of these same traits or feelings in yourself. You can learn to respond in ways that enable you to keep moving toward all you are seeking to accomplish. By becoming familiar with the signs and steps to overcome any manner of internal challenge, you will possess the final piece to unlock your relentless determination.

Understanding Impostor Syndrome

The term "impostor phenomenon" was first introduced in 1978 in the article "The Impostor Phenomenon in High Achieving Women: Dynamics and Therapeutic Intervention" by Dr. Pauline R. Clance and Dr. Suzanne A. Imes. Since then, many studies, journals, and books have been written about Impostor Syndrome, giving us a better understanding of its characteristics and strategies to limit the effects of any internal obstacles it causes.

Struggles with Impostor Syndrome are extremely common. According to a review article published in the *International Journal of Behavioral Science*, 70% of people experience Impostor Syndrome in their lives.

Key Indicators of Impostor Syndrome are:
1. Repetition of the impostor cycle
2. The need to be special or the best
3. Characteristics of Superman/Superwoman
4. Fear of failure
5. Denial of ability and discounting praise
6. Feeling guilty about your success

1. Repetition of the Impostor Cycle – When assigned a task, you may feel doubt about being able to complete it or to do it well. This results in either procrastination of over-preparing.

- **Procrastination** – A sense of anxiety about doing well at the task starts to serve as a blockade for even getting started. Of

course, procrastination just means less time to complete the task and the need to scramble to finish on time.
- **Over-preparing** – The habit of spending hours, days, even weeks researching the best ways to complete the task, all in the name of eliminating mistakes and failure. Except for the failure of never starting the task in the first place.

ASK YOURSELF –

- When given an important task, do you delay getting started or find yourself doing inordinate amounts of research, often resulting in delays?
- Do you avoid starting a new project because of feelings that you lack the needed skills?

2. The need to be special or the best – Impostors will often feel they must be doing something special or better than their peers to be seen as equals.

ASK YOURSELF –

- Do you often compare your skills to those of your peers?
- Do you see yourself as "competing" against those in the same job as you?

3. Characteristics of Superman/Superwoman – Impostors frequently set extremely high expectations for themselves, resulting in a pattern of moving from one stressful situation to another. They see mistakes as personal failures, not learning moments. To compensate "weakness," impostors tend to overwork and take on much more than others.

ASK YOURSELF –

- Are you a perfectionist?
- Do you take on more because of feeling you do not measure up?

4. Fear of failure – Impostors have a poorly aligned relationship with failure. Any mistake may finally expose them as a fraud. Fear of failure often drives an impostor to overprepare and overwork.

ASK YOURSELF –

- Do you feel the failure of a task or project will expose your lack of skills?
- To avoid failure at any cost, do you overwork and overprepare regardless of the level of stress it causes?

5. Denial of ability and discounting praise – A hallmark of Impostor Syndrome. Despite external evidence of their competence, Impostors dismiss accolades and praise while remaining convinced that they do not deserve all they have achieved.

ASK YOURSELF –

- When receiving praise for a key sale, do you respond, "I guess we all get lucky sometimes?"
- When a coworker thanks you for hard work, do you discount the work involved or feel compelled to immediately thank them for his or her work?

6. Feeling guilty about your success – Impostors feel fear or guilt about the success they may have, often feeling they "didn't really earn" that success. Impostors avoid sharing accomplishments with family and friends, feeling embarrassed to have more.

ASK YOURSELF –

- Do you avoid telling your siblings about a promotion you received because you believe they are more deserving?
- Do you hide the fact you just closed a big sale at work, one you had been working on for 18 months, simply out of fear that your friends will think you get all the lucky break while they struggle?

Do you see yourself in any of the six traits above or recognize any of the thought patterns? Impostors frequently beat themselves up about their perceived shortcomings or are harder on themselves than most, expecting perfection. If you found yourself saying "Yes" to several of the questions you just read, it is time for you to be honest with yourself by admitting that you are a Grade A, Numero Uno, Bona Fide Impostor. Take your seat at the table. **You are in great company.**

Overcoming the Internal Challenge

If you recognize yourself in the traits reviewed, you are not doomed to a life of fear and desperation. Instead, Impostor Syndrome should be thought of as a set of characteristics that have no reason to hold you back. You may never completely get rid of it. However, by recognizing those feelings and understand the strategies with which to respond, you learn to quickly deal with the feelings and keep charging forward. This means you can and *should* live a life filled with confidence, growth, and fulfillment.

Many highly successful people have admitted to struggling with these same feelings. Names you will recognize like Tom Hanks, Supreme Court Justice Sonia Sotomayor, Starbucks CEO Howard Schultz, poet and activist Maya Angelou, and Meryl Streep. This list represents only a small fraction of successful people who have admitted their feelings of impostorism. Even former first lady Michelle Obama recently shared, "I still have Impostor Syndrome from time to time." Most of us would agree that Meryl Streep and Michelle Obama have done well for themselves, despite occasionally dealing with feelings of being an impostor. This means that you are not alone and the sky is the limit for you!

Now that you know what traits to look for, it is time to understand the steps you can take to quiet the impostor's voice inside you and replace it with confidence and determination.

Steps to overcome Impostor Syndrome:

1. Start by calling the impostor by name
2. Share your feelings with others
3. List your unique strengths
4. Acknowledge praise and accomplishments

Step 1 – Start by calling the impostor by name – Impostor syndrome lurks in the dark places in your mind, hanging out in the same circles as fear and shame. Banish the impostor by calling awareness to it. Acknowledge that it exists within you (as we learned, it lives within most of us). I recommend to my clients they literally give it a name. Who can be afraid of a Fred or an Ethel? The next time that voice of doubt pops up, take away its power with, "Oh, Fred, you are talking like a fool again." Another option is to counteract any negative voice by creating an inner voice that emboldens you with energy and confidence. For example, Grammy Award-winning singer Beyoncé has named her onstage persona "Sasha Fierce." Pick whatever name gives you the power to dismiss undesirable thoughts.

Step 2 – Share your feelings with others – The idea of telling others may seem terrifying at first, but you will soon find many others who have these same internal struggles. With change and complexity happening so frequently, most people are feeling high levels of doubt. Adding in the uncertainty caused by today's global events, many of us are feeling uncomfortable and on the edge of being overwhelmed. Share those feelings with trusted friends and peers. **Knowing you are not alone will give you strength and confidence.**

Step 3 – Create a list of your unique strengths – Recognize your strengths instead of any perceived shortcomings. No one, not even the most accomplished salespeople, leaders, and speakers can do it all. Nor do you have to do it all, either. Address skill gaps by asking for help and seeking out knowledge. As you do, emphasize the skills and capabilities at which you excel by using them to serve others.

Step 4 – Acknowledge praise and accomplishment – Celebrate accomplishments and accept recognition and words of praise. Never diminish your effort by deflecting praise or immediately heaping praise back on the person recognizing what you have achieved. From this moment forward, when someone acknowledges your contributions, say "Thank you," while taking in what she is saying. **Take deliberate time to *feel* the recognition of your hard work, thoughtfulness, and impact on others. You earned it.**

Note—Much of what we do in our careers and community is the result of team contributions. This means that some may feel uncomfortable accepting praise while not immediately giving credit to team contributions. I am not suggesting you take all the credit. I am simply suggesting that you not downplay your role in the accomplishments by deflecting praise to the team. If appropriate, first acknowledge your own work with something as simple as, "Thank you." Let that moment sit, then add, "There were many of us who worked hard to make this deal happen. Mary and Jim were tremendous partners on this. It is a win for all of us." Finding the balance between appropriately sharing the praise while never missing a chance to give yourself a mental High Five!

 **Success Step**

Make a list of your strengths. Write 5-8 strengths, traits, and habits you already have in place today that will help you reach Invincible. If that comes easy to you, try for 10-15. Think about the strengths you have shown in both your current role and past roles. Are you an innovative thinker, a great communicator, or a strong team player? Are you organized, tenacious, or open-minded? Also, think outside of your career to other parts of your life. Are you a great mother, father, husband, wife, or grandparent? Do you have empathy for others? Write down everything you can think of today and continue to update the list as you think of more strengths.

Once you have the list created, stick it up near your workstation, on the bathroom mirror, or anywhere it will easily be seen. Read over the list at least twice a day. Soon you will be able to repeat the list to yourself at any time. As you do, you are reinforcing those strengths and making negative self-talk slide away.

If any of the traits related to Impostor Syndrome are limiting your ability to push through a challenge, use the four steps outlined in this section to overcome those internal challenges while building more positive behaviors. As developing these new skills and responses to internal challenge takes time, create weekly or bi-weekly reminders to do a self-assessment of your progress. Are you focusing more on your strengths? Is the impostor's voice easily dismissed? By adding structure, you become purposeful in using these steps and making adjustments where necessary.

The Danger of Complacency

After reading through the common signs of Impostor Syndrome, you may be thinking, "I don't have that. Those traits did not describe me." That's great. **The principles in this book will build on everything you are already experiencing in your thriving sales or leadership career.**

Another common internal challenge I often see in clients is not recognizing a need to change. Too often, the catalyst for change is when someone hits rock bottom. Until that lowest point, people can find themselves stuck with no forward momentum. It is as if they are treading water. They tell themselves that they will make a change after one life event or another. Maybe they need to wait for the kids to get into college or wait until a spouse finishes his or her degree. They tell themselves that changing to a fulfilling job is impossible because it pays less money. Whatever the reasoning, it all adds up to not pushing themselves ahead in a way that reflects their full potential.

This typically results in making vague goals, then not holding yourself accountable. People like this often fool themselves by saying that they are being selfless. They are putting the kids, spouse, or partner first. They make a sick mom or dying aunt a priority. Maybe they put their career first, while letting their relationships falter. Without a low point, there is no need to make a change. They just keep treading water, stagnant in that same spot. Day after day becomes month after month and then year after year. Though they may not be struggling with Impostor Syndrome, they are struggling with an internal challenge that is equally limiting: complacency.

Complacency is the death of a thousand cuts. Even worse, they are cuts we give to ourselves. We are satisfied because we are not articulating, "I am not capable." Instead, we justify our position by expressing, "I'm not capable right now." Let me tell you right now, the result of those two sentences is the same.

All around us, every day, there are people who are building a career they love while their kids are still young, their spouses are finishing their degrees, and family members are sick. They are changing to fulfilling jobs and adjusting their spending to afford the cut in pay. Others are starting a side hustle while remaining in their current careers. Every single day, people no more put together than you, with an equal number of questions, fears, and obstacles, are doing exactly what you want to do. **Now it is your turn.**

Your goal is not just to get by. You are here to reach greatness! You can lead a life that is safe, simple, and steady. Another option, the best option, is to live a life that fills you with confidence and purpose. A life where you seek out chances to impact others. One that makes you want to stand up, raise your fists in the air and shout, "**I AM INVINCIBLE!**"

Do not allow complacency to stop you from reaching your dreams. Before they were celebrities and businesspeople with names that we all recognize, the people I have highlighted in this chapter were once exactly where you are today. They had dreams and visions of success, just like you. They also had many doubts and insecurities, just like you. If they developed the driving force to ignore any negative self-talk, you can, too!

Focus on movement and progress, pushing yourself to reach higher than most. You will find those internal voices of doubt and wonky reasons that have kept you stuck will start to fade away. **By pushing through internal challenge and complacency, you develop the relentless determination needed to reach your dreams.**

INVINCIBLE TIPS

1. Make a list of 5-8 unique strengths
2. Keep your list handy, reading it each day
3. Learn to dismiss negative self-talk because it has no power in your life
4. Focus on growth and impacting others today
5. Watch out for complacency that may be keeping you stuck in place

SUMMARY

Many of us, at some point in our lives, have struggled with self-doubt. Even the most skilled and seemingly successful among us are not immune to negative voices that attempt to derail us from our goals. By knowing what to look for, you can identify common characteristics that may indicate you may be experiencing Impostor Syndrome. Once identified, acknowledge that you are not alone. Next, remind yourself daily of your unique strengths and areas where you shine. Learn to take in fully the words of recognition and accomplishment, as you have earned them. Finally, do not allow complacency to keep you from achieving growth. Commit to progress each day. Find new ways to serve, new ways to learn, new ways to have an impact on others. Quiet any internal voices of doubt by taking consistent action toward your goals.

Make the voice of determination be the voice you hear!

INVINCIBLE PRINCIPLE 1: CREATE INTENTIONAL CONNECTION

*"The connections we make in the course of a
life – maybe that's what heaven is."*
— Fred Rogers

You have now unlocked the relentless determination you will use to reach your sales and leadership goals. With that in place, it is time to transition to the proven process that will catapult you to success. This is the same methodology I used throughout my sales and leadership career and is now used by the clients and organizations with whom I work. Even today, I still use these same steps to ensure I am setting myself up to create the best possible outcomes for my customer and team member interactions. You, too, will achieve exceptional results when you utilize the six Invincible Principles.

As you learn the Invincible Principles, you will discover that they are best used together. For them to be most effective, they have a certain amount of dependency on each other. Granted, improving the skills outlined in any one principle will yield positive results. However, each additional principle you utilize will act as a force multiplier in your customer interactions and in your career. That is especially true with Invincible Principles 1 and 2. These first two principles go hand in hand with each other, as if they were Gemini twins. By strengthening your skills in both areas, you release the full power of their collective strength.

Do you recall what my coworker Michael (the sales legend) said to me after that first miserable sales year, when I asked him what his secret was to excel in sales? He said, "Stop trying to be great at sales. Become great at serving your customer." Serving is at the heart of sales. It is also at the heart of good leadership, confident public speaking, and a happy personal life. The more we focus on serving others, the more impact we have, and the more fulfilled we will be. To serve effectively, we must first have a connection with the other person. If I have no connection to you, I really have my work cut out for me to serve you effectively. **This leads to Invincible Principle 1: Create Intentional Connection.**

Take a moment to think back. More than likely, you have had experiences with salespeople who tried to sell you something way before you had any connection with them, right? Can you remember a time when that happened? Perhaps you felt they rushed right to the sale? Or you felt they tried to create a connection that was fake? They acted like you had been best friends for years when you had just met for the first time 10 minutes earlier. Have you had experiences like that? If so, how did that interaction make you feel? More than likely, it made you more than a little uncomfortable.

During my keynote speeches, I ask audience members to recall a bad sales situation where they felt the salesperson rushed into the sale or tried to do something fake. I will ask them to share with me what images come to mind when they think of these experiences. Invariably, almost every time, audience member's hands shoot in the air and someone cannot wait to shout out, "Used car salesman!" Those pushy salespeople that pounce on you as soon as you step out of your car. Of course, this perception is not true of all used car salespeople. I have met very nice, patient, and skilled used car salespeople out there in the world. It is a fact that many people have reservations about buying a car simply because of this perception. It serves as an important reminder for you to stay mindful of the importance of patience and sincerity when developing relationships.

Instead, despite everyone seemingly being in a rush nowadays, take your time creating a real connection with your customers. Even in sales careers such as cars, retail, mobile sales, and others, you must find ways of building connections with those you are hoping to serve. How do you know what a real connection looks like? At the very least, the connection you are striving for is a two-way connection. Not just one direction. **That means they are sharing with you as much or more than you are telling them.**

That was the biggest issue in my first year in sales. My manager told me to go out and sell, so I went out and pushed, and pushed, and pushed. I thought, "If I just get to enough of my customers and tell them about my products, eventually someone will buy." My marketing team gave me a slick PowerPoint deck filled with interesting facts and figures. I set up countless customer meetings to share those facts and figures. The problem was, it was just me telling my customers something or trying to get something from them—their money. It was all one way, meaning I was never creating real connections. You can easily avoid my rookie mistake by taking some simple steps to connect with the people you are trying to serve.

LEARNING TO LISTEN AS YOU LISTEN TO LEARN

If you want to form connections with customers, you need to take the time to learn who they are, their likes and dislikes. What are their goals and challenges? Your customers must feel as if you have a real understanding of the things they care about. In sales, that means you need to understand their business and their key problems. For leaders, the same needs to be true about your employees. Yes, it is true that the larger your team or company, the more difficult it is to know everyone on a personal level. However, you should be expected to understand each of your team members' roles and responsibilities, along with their pain points.

If you speak in front of a group, the more people you are speaking to, the more difficult it is to form individual connections. By developing a deeper understanding of the various groups of people in the room, to the extent possible, the more successful you will be. That is why your first goal for any meeting, any interaction with those you hope to serve is to learn. It is paramount to identify their needs accurately and completely. The more you can know the specific challenges of the people you are striving to serve, the better you can serve them. **Remember this: In sales, if you want to earn, first you must learn.** The same is true for leaders and speakers.

Learning requires what key skill? Listening, of course. It is impossible for you to learn when you are talking. The more you can keep your mouth closed and instead focus on learning, the greater the connection you will form with the person with whom you are having the conversation. Most of us feel we are great listeners. Unfortunately, this is often not the case. Too often, when someone else is speaking, what are we doing? We are thinking of our response, right? We are formulating our reply and just waiting for the moment the person takes a breath so we can jump in! In another common scenario, someone is speaking to us and he mentions something familiar or interesting, so we immediately start recalling our own story and experience. We cannot wait to tell our own story based on what he just shared instead of staying in listening mode.

 Success Step

Instead of listening with the intent to hear, your goal should be listening to understand. One great thing to try–imagine that you are to be tested on your listening by repeating and comprehending what someone has just said. If that were true, would you pass the test most of the time? If this is an area where you frequently struggle, try this test and see how you do.

After your next conversation with someone, take a few minutes to write down as much as you can remember of what she said. If she is someone with whom you are comfortable, ask her to look over what you wrote. How close are you to what she said? Did you accurately remember the most important things she shared? Beyond just the data points, can you describe how she was feeling about what she shared? Make your goal in any conversation to focus intently on understanding both the key thoughts and feelings of the other person.

This leads to the next key connection step: develop empathy. Understanding is important, but putting yourself in their shoes will build the deepest connection. Empathy helps you feel the pain of their challenges or fears. If you feel their pain, you are in a far better position to know how you can help them. Once you truly experience their challenges and needs, you can respond back to them in a way that makes them feel heard.

In his book *Just Listen,* author Mark Goulston takes this a step further. He encourages us to make the other person feel "felt" in a sincere way. This can be done by repeating back what you heard, which includes emotion statements. "I understand that it is very frustrating for you to have to call our customer support. It makes you angry because you feel nothing is being resolved," or "Thank you for sharing with me that you don't understand how our team contributes to the success of the company. I would imagine that's confusing and a little scary for you." If the person with whom you are speaking feels that you "felt" their pain, he is much more inclined to let his guard down, share even more, and thus be more connected. Please note: to avoid sounding condescending to the other person, only use this technique with genuine empathy toward his or her feelings.

As a former Microsoft employee, I had a world-class exposure to the power of empathy when Satya Nadella took over as CEO in 2014. In its earliest days, Microsoft was ultra-competitive, both inside and outside the organization. Externally, we were incentivized to beat out the competition. This mentality puts the focus on winning and not on your customer's specific needs. Internally, this same competitive drive caused problems. Various teams did not share enough information with each other about products and projects they were working on. This led to frustration and disparity of experiences for the customer. As a result, the company stagnated after a decade of losing market share in most of its core businesses.

When Satya took over, he immediately began talking about the importance of listening with empathy. He called it "the key source of business innovation." His coaching taught us that listening with empathy was "paramount to our ability to grasp customers' unmet, unarticulated needs." He led by example, which helped reinforce the shift in culture. Product teams started collaborating in new ways because they felt safer to share information. Leadership started emphasizing the need for listening with empathy during group training and 1:1 coaching sessions. Salespeople took it to heart, embracing the importance of listening first. It is hard to argue the results. With Satya at the helm, Microsoft has had phenomenal growth, defined by new partnerships, improved relationships, and ecstatic customers. They are currently enjoying the highest sales in company history, which has even past skeptics agreeing it may be one of the biggest organizational turnarounds in business history.

How to Ask

To go along with listening, you must get very good at asking questions. I can only imagine the eye rolls of those of you reading this thinking, "Really? Now you want me to practice asking questions?" Resoundingly, yes! This is often another area that people take for granted. I cannot possibly be the only colleague, friend, or family member to walk away from a long conversation with someone shaking my head as I realize, "They didn't ask me a single question about myself." We've all experienced one-sided conversations. Even if we have been asked questions, are they good ones? Remember, your goal for every meeting is to learn more about those you serve, regardless of whether they are customers, team members, or a sampling of your audience. Asking good questions will ensure you learn as much as you can in a very short period of time.

Yes, we have all been asking questions of each other for a very long time. However, just because we have spent a lifetime asking each other questions, that does not mean we are good asking the *right* questions. **The right questions take deliberate thought and intention. What information do you need that will help you to serve this individual better?** Our goal is to get the other person to reveal more about herself or the challenges that she is facing. We also want to understand what success means to her, so we know when we are achieving it. Is she understanding us in the way in which we intend or does she need more information? That is why taking deliberate time to focus on asking questions is so important.

The better you get at asking questions, the more effective your interactions will be. Asking questions demonstrates to your customer, team, or audience member that you are there not just to get what you want. Instead, you are there to learn. Additionally, asking questions puts the focus on them and takes it off yourself. This will be good news for anyone who gets nervous in meetings or speaking in front of others. By taking the focus off yourself and putting it on them where it belongs, it could be just what you are looking for to feel empowered and in control.

 SUCCESS STEP

How do you get good at asking questions? Just like listening, it takes practice. In fact, I suggest you set aside intentional time to do just that. Take five minutes a day to think of questions to ask those you serve. Set a timer for yourself. Put it on your calendar each day. You decide if it works best for you to do it in the morning, before the craziness of your day, or at the end of your day just before going home for the night. Pick whatever time works well for you, then stick to it.

Sometimes you may identify general questions that you can ask many of your customers, team members, or clients. Other questions will be appropriate for one single individual. The key intent is for you to learn more about them, which will help you better serve. Beyond just thinking of questions, it is important to write the questions down. The questions can be copied into your favorite app of choice like Evernote, OneNote, or just into a reminders list. The place you choose should be easily accessible on your phone so that you can quickly refer to the questions when needed. Too often, we think of questions and never write them down. In the busyness of conducting a meeting, we struggle to remember the questions we wanted to ask. Taking the additional step of writing them in a favorite app will avoid this frustrating experience.

SOME OF MY FAVORITE QUESTIONS TO ASK:

- What are you hoping to accomplish in the next year?
- What is something your favorite vendor is doing that you wished all of your vendors did?
- Do you struggle with (insert common pain point here)?
- What do you enjoy most/least about your career?
- In what ways can I serve you better?
- As you look at the next six months, what are some of the ways in which you are looking to grow?
- Is there a recent example where we have not met your expectation?
- A few months from now, when we are celebrating our success, what will I have done to help you make that happen?

There are many more questions to consider asking, depending on whether you are addressing a customer, team member, or speaking to a live audience. However, the more you diligently focus on making sure that you are asking questions, the more opportunity you will have to learn about those you serve.

Note–It may seem silly to sit and write down questions to ask. The skeptic in you may balk at wasting these precious five minutes.

However, as listening is so important to establishing connection, and asking good questions is the key to listening, the time you spend is an investment in your success.

When I started running at almost 50 years old, everyone told me I needed to stretch before and after my daily jogs. Since it added 20 minutes to my routine, I often skipped the stretching, thinking I was fine. Within a few months, I was feeling discomfort in my left hamstring that would last throughout the day. "It'll work itself out if I just keep pushing." Fast forward 6 months, I had to stop running because I was in so much discomfort every day. Now I have gone through months of physical therapy and a near-daily focus on stretching, which still has not completely resolved the issue. Looking back, if I had just taken those extra 20 minutes for each run, it would have saved me over a year of continuous discomfort. Think of writing down your questions each day as your stretching routine. It is the time you spend "warming up" that will make sure your meetings and presentations are pain-free and filled with connection and impact.

Become a Master Discoverer

I have been to many events or meetings where no one seems curious about getting to know me. Sure, plenty of people have talked to me, but far too often, they have only spoken about themselves. Most of us have been to events where we have had multiple conversations, and the people with whom we are speaking keep the focus on themselves. I call these people "me-monsters." All the focus is about "me, me, me!" If all of us have experienced this, that means there are way too many people out there not asking questions or taking a genuine interest in getting to know others.

Asking questions and listening are key elements to establishing a connection. Too often, we let this slip. After all, we have a job to do. Sometimes we are in a hurry to get through this meeting because we have five more meetings we need to get to that day. Sometimes we are too focused on our own objectives for any given meeting or conversation. Sometimes we only want to charge through our prepared content, worried that if we start asking questions, that encourages the customer to ask questions that may derail our content. However, remind yourself, **content is not connection.**

Yes, we will always have a newer version of our products, services, or updates we want to share. As leaders, we have team objectives, quotas, and company updates to deliver. As speakers, we will have new stories, new messages, and new ideas to articulate. All of that is important, *after* the connection. If we stop pushing ourselves to understand more about the people we are hoping to serve, they will surely lose sight of us.

Michael Van Cleave, a Director of Cybersecurity and Modern Workplace, shared with me something he reinforces with his team on a regular basis. He pushes his team to think of themselves as "Master Discoverers." Michael schedules time for his team to get together and role-play the process of asking questions. He encourages his team to prepare by writing questions down in advance, highlighting those questions they thought to ask their customers that resulted in the customer making a discovery. Team members then practice asking these questions to each other so that the group is continuously learning from each other.

Whether a seller, leader, or speaker, think of yourself as a "Master Discoverer." Not only should you be challenging yourself to five minutes a day of dedicated time to write down questions, but you should also be looking for other ways to practice. If this is an area of discomfort for you, push yourself to approach others and ask questions at family or work events. If needed, turn it into a game. Tell yourself, "I'm not allowed to leave the event until I have learned two interesting facts about at least three people."

At first, this may seem to take a great deal of effort. In no time, it will be more natural and enjoyable. You will appreciate your ability to get people to share information about themselves while preparing yourself for those customer situations where connection really matters. Think of it as filling a basket. What are you taking home after these events? What is in your basket?

Ultimately, you need to be asking the questions that will best help you be successful at serving. We must strive for deeper perspectives and insights. Nick Carr, a VP at AvePoint, an award-winning service provider in Chicago, trains his team to utilize "The 3 Whys" of questioning. This is the practice of digging deep enough to answer "Why?" three times. For example, if you are told by a customer, "We need better reporting," your response is, "Why do you need that?" They may respond, "So we have better visibility into our monthly financials." To which you respond, "Why is more visibility important?" They may respond, "We need to better identify trends in our business." Once again, you go deeper by asking, "Why is it important to see those trends?" Their response may be "By seeing sales trends in real-time, our executives can better understand how resources can be allocated to maximize effectiveness." Instead of your goal being to deliver on the vague (i.e., easily defunded) "Better Reporting" project, you now have a front seat to the strategic (i.e., funded) "Real-time Executive Reporting for Sales Excellence" project—Gold!

Two final notes when it comes to asking questions and listening. First, not everyone we speak to will be able to provide the valuable insights we need to succeed. **You must continuously assess whether you are asking questions of the right person or if you need to be talking to others.** A general rule of thumb, the closer you are to the person responsible for approving funds, the more likely it is he or she are the ones you need to approach. Chris Ross, a National Sales Director at Perficient, shared a story about Steve. Steve was a highly regarded account executive, well-liked by his customers. He built fantastic relationships. However, Chris found that although Steve's customers were always attending the dinners and social events Steve planned, he struggled to reach his sales targets. It turns out that though Steve cultivated great relationships within the accounts, those relationships were not the people making the decision. Steve was great at serving… a free meal. Make sure the people you are pushing to serve are the ones who can best make the decisions you are looking to be made.

Secondly, remember all this asking and listening is to build a better connection. Do not get stuck in asking questions only about the challenges someone faces. Though understanding that is important to your ability to serve, make sure you are a well-rounded "Master Discoverer." Take a genuine interest in getting to know them. Are they married, what hobbies do they enjoy, how many kids do they have? Not only will you discover common interests, but it may also give you an opportunity to reference some of this personal connection later during your presentation or future meetings. With all this newfound connection, you can rest assured there will be future meetings!

INVINCIBLE TIPS

1. Great connection comes from great listening and great questions
2. Develop empathy for those you serve
3. If you want to earn, first you must learn
4. Beyond listening to hear, strive to listen to understand deeply

SUMMARY

Listening with empathy and asking questions are two essential components to establishing a connection with those we serve. Most of us know this, yet too often we are not nearly as good or as deliberate at this as we should be. Always in a hurry, we barge into meetings with our own agendas. We are eager to get through the 30 slides it took hours to prepare. Avoid this pitfall by reminding yourself before every customer interaction that you are there to learn. You are there to learn more about your customer, their business, and their needs. Setting a goal to be always striving to grow your connection, as both a seller and a leader, will ensure you are putting your customer needs ahead of your own. The more your customer shares with you, the more you will align your solution to meet her or his needs. Let the meeting be all about them. After all, isn't it (and shouldn't it always be)?

If I want to serve, I need to connect. If I want to connect, I need to learn. If I want to learn, I need to listen.

INVINCIBLE PRINCIPLE 2: BUILD LASTING TRUST

"If people like you, they'll listen to you. But if they trust you, they'll do business with you."
— Zig Ziglar

To go along with intentional connection, we must have another important factor in place to serve others. More than likely, you have heard the common expression, "People do business with people they know, like, and trust." Because it is a required part of business, let's understand how to strengthen the bond with our customers by walking through **Invincible Principle 2: Build Lasting Trust**.

Any successful relationship needs both Principles 1 and 2 working together. **This is because it is impossible to have connection without trust.** In our personal lives, most would agree that our deepest relationships need these two qualities. What about in our careers? Just as outside of the workplace, to achieve the highest levels of success in business, those we serve must be able to rely confidently on our shared partnership.

Author Stephen Covey said it well: "Trust is the glue of life. It's the foundational principle that holds all relationships." Take a moment and think about this statement. Most salespeople and leaders would agree that establishing trust is essential. Yet even for those who are not in a sales role or who may never strive for a leadership position, the importance of building trust should not be overlooked. *Whenever* you are speaking to someone, trying to share an idea, or move him to take an action you need him to take, that will not happen if he does not have faith you.

Top organizations know the importance of this. Yet just because it is a line in your mission statement, do not expect that it can be a checkbox exercise. Before becoming Managing Director of Healthcare & Life Sciences at Alphabet, Chris Sakalosky ran a multi-billion business at Microsoft. He shared, "The biggest challenge you have is trust. It is so tough to gain, easily lost, and nearly impossible to win back."

Remember, our overarching goal is to serve others. To do that, we need to know where the problems are. Instead of blindly throwing out solutions, or worse, making assumptions about challenges other people may be experiencing, we need to get to the truth for that individual. Employees and customers are far more likely to share the issues they are facing if they feel that you are someone that can help them find the right solution.

How can we get others to have confidence in us? Simon Sinek, author of the bestselling book *Start With Why*, explains, "You can't teach people trust. Trust is a feeling. Like all feelings, trust must be earned. It evolves." Not only is it a feeling that must be earned, but it is also temporary. This means that we must reestablish trust on an ongoing basis. To enable this, I suggest you make it a part of your customer interactions by utilizing four key traits. To make these traits easy to remember, I have created this formula: **T=A+C+I+R,** or **Trust = Ability + Consistency + Integrity + Responsibility**. Let's take a closer look at how these four traits work together to convey trustworthiness.

Your Ability Is Your Credibility

Trust is based on credibility. Without credibility, there is little chance that anyone you are speaking to is ever going to feel comfortable doing business with you, follow your lead, or even pay attention during one of your presentations. Fortunately, some level of credibility is afforded to you without any additional effort on your part. Most often, other people consider you to have a certain amount of credibility just by the nature of you having the position in the company that you do. They figure, "If Company A hired her, she must be qualified." That is not to say that you did not work hard to get hired by Company A, it is just that you generally have a certain level of credibility based on your customer's understanding and respect for your company itself. That small amount of credibility from your employer's credentials only gets you in the door, if you are lucky. You must make a conscious effort to grow your credibility beyond your job title. **The surest way to do that is by enhancing and demonstrating your ability.**

Ability is a culmination of your unique combination of knowledge, skills, and general get-things-done-*ness*. It comes from a deep understanding of your customers and the offerings of your organization. It is your blend of competencies, such as how you interact with others, adapt to rapid change, cultivate a sense of shared outcomes, and motivate others to act. It also comes from your work product, such as the content you create, the challenges you overcome, and the relationships you improve. In other words, ability is what makes you the goal-crushing, problem-solving, results-oriented expert that you are.

There are so many ways you can take action to improve your expertise and skills. Oftentimes, the ways in which you further develop your ability is dependent on your individual role and existing experience. The methods you will use to enhance your ability will be different based on your industry, organization, leadership, or team needs. Given this, let us review ways in which you can *demonstrate* your ability.

Are you someone who prefers to sit back quietly and let others discover your talents? Do you consider yourself someone who thinks, "I let my work speak for itself"? I get it. I was, too. Unfortunately, as sellers, leaders, and speakers, we cannot rely on understated success. This is because of several reasons. First, being good at what we do is the baseline expectation. Remember, to differentiate ourselves, we must stand out from others, not blend in. **It is not enough to sit back, hoping people recognize your expertise. You must make it known.**

Customers and hiring managers are doing their homework. A December 2018 article on jobs site Glassdoor speaks to the common practice of a hiring manager to review a potential candidate's social media content. Without question, your current and future customers are, too. This has been confirmed to me time and time again when I meet a new customer or client and they say, "You look just like your LinkedIn picture!" **Because your customers are using social platforms to learn more about you, they have become a simple yet effective way to demonstrate your depth of knowledge long before you walk in the door.**

What can you do about this? There are so many different platforms available today that you can leverage to demonstrate your ability. I mentioned that one of the leading platforms, from a professional perspective, is LinkedIn. With over 675 million active users and growing, LinkedIn is an important tool to showcase your knowledge and to build trust. One of the easiest places to start is to keep your profile up to date. Add links to your organization's website or where customers can go for more information about your unique offering. A very underutilized feature is LinkedIn Recommendations. Think of these recommendations as mini testimonials. Make it a point to be asking for them from your customers and peers, as well as giving them to others. When asking for someone to write a recommendation for you, include suggestions on areas of your work you would like to highlight. When done well, these recommendations build trust by showing others that you are someone with whom they want to do business.

While an updated profile and recommendations are important, sharing content is one of the easiest ways to demonstrate ability. In my sales and leadership consulting, clients will often ask, "Why should I even bother posting content online?" The answer is because of the opportunity. There are over 675 million active users on LinkedIn alone. Only a small percentage of users are creating and posting content. This means that one of the fastest ways to stand out and establish expertise is posting content and engaging with another person's content. Start sharing articles, text posts, images, and videos, all related to your area of knowledge. Equally important, engage with others on the platform who are posting content to which you can lend insight. Connect with current and potential customers, other leaders, possible mentors, and anyone you feel will be a source of information and engagement. Join groups that are relevant to your line of work or areas of expertise. Once you join, make it a point to contribute.

LinkedIn is only one of the platforms available on which you can share your expertise. Creating a YouTube channel, Facebook group, or podcast are examples of the myriad of other options you should consider. As they have for me, these platforms will increase the number of clients, referrals, testimonials, speaking opportunities, collaborations, and in-person conversations that come to you as you share your ability with others.

As much as I encourage these external platforms for you to leverage, I understand not everyone will feel comfortable posting online. To that, I have two responses: First, I strongly suggest you *get* used to it. According to Statista (statista.com/statistics/278414/number-of-worldwide-social-network-users/), the number of social media users is expected to grow beyond 3.4 billion people by 2023. This presents a far too customer-rich environment for you not to be utilizing. When you decide only the marketing team should care about social media, you are missing a marquee chance to establish your expertise on platforms your customers are using to find information and build trust with potential vendors.

Second, if you just cannot bring yourself to post content and share your expertise publicly via social media, start by finding ways of doing it internally. In your organization, look for opportunities to join internal planning and development groups, discussion forums, or anywhere you can share your knowledge and experiences with others. For those ready to do more speaking, one of the fastest ways to demonstrate your ability is by leading internal or external training sessions. If there is not a routine training program established, explore starting one yourself. Not only will you be demonstrating your ability, but you will also be adding value to others.

Given all the ways I have listed that you can demonstrate ability, everyone will soon be singing your praises, even more than they already are today. Yet I saved the simplest idea for last. **The simplest way for you to actively demonstrate your ability is by speaking up.** Alisa Swann, one of the most inspiring leaders for whom I have had the pleasure to work, says, "It is so easy to go into that next meeting without preparing, yet so important that you go in instead ready to add value."

All of us are moving super-fast, with too much on our plates. It is easy to race between meetings, hoping we do not fall asleep or hoping the meeting ends early so that we can get back to our work. Instead, do not miss an opportunity to go in prepared to contribute or, at the very least, to be wide-eyed and ready to add our own value to the subject at hand. **Remember, it is up to you to ensure your customers, leadership team, and others have a full understanding of your knowledge, skills, and abilities.**

CONSISTENCY IS KEY

As you will learn in Chapter 6, I am a huge fan of creative and innovative solutions. Today, your ability to pivot quickly to a new approach is invaluable. We all get stuck, run into setbacks, or discover that those decisions we were sure were right did not go our way. Your willingness to pivot to something new or to rally your team around new ideas will give you more chances to succeed versus sticking to a plan long after it should have been abandoned. This means that there is a huge benefit to innovative thinking and your ability to work through different methods of going after success. While mental and organizational agility is essential, **to build trust, you must have consistency.**

Inspirational speaker Tony Robbins shares, "It's not what we do once in a while that shapes our lives. It's what we do consistently." Tony's words are relevant not just to those striving to improve their own lives, but for those who are striving to improve the lives of others. **Customers and employees feel more comfortable trusting someone that they can count on consistently.** They are looking for a vendor or leader to be there to answer questions, offer guidance, and provide information when it is needed. Inconsistent and unreliable salespeople only contact their customers when *they* need something, such as when they have a new product, update, or promotion to discuss. Through regular meetings or communications, a reliable, consistent salesperson will be frequently checking in with his customers, keeping their finger on the pulse of his customers' needs and ensuring those needs are being addressed.

Leaders cannot afford to be inconsistent with employees, either. One of the least reliable and confusing managers in my career had the maddening habit of canceling our monthly one-on-ones, often an hour before we were scheduled to meet. When we did meet, I never knew what to expect from the experience. Some monthly meetings would consist of little more than me watching her eat her lunch as she occasionally asked me questions about my various sales opportunities. Randomly, without notice, some meetings would be her asking me what I was doing to further the development in my career or how I was progressing in my yearly stretch goals. Since I had no idea what to expect from any of these meetings, I often overprepared for everything. This added to my frustration as she seemed not to have prepared at all. As you can imagine, I could not wait for them to be over. How much trust do you think I had in my manager?

How do you develop consistency with your customers or team members? First and foremost, your communication cadence should be in line with your customer's and employee's needs. I suggest checking in at least once a month; however, this can be fluid, depending on the time of year and what may be going on. Is your customer in the middle of a big project utilizing your products? They may need additional hand-holding and want to hear from you once or twice a week. Are they heads-down in their end-of-year push? They may need lots of space and do not want anything other than urgent communications during this period. Work with them to establish the appropriate rhythm.

Second, any schedule you create must be something that you can maintain. Do not make a big deal about setting up consistent meetings with an employee or customer, only to miss expectations month after month. Careful thought and planning can make it manageable and useful for both parties.

It is worth noting that consistency in your interactions with customers and employees will also result in achieving consistent results. Gary Angotti, a high-performance sales director, notes that real success is not about putting a few wins together once or twice. Your goal is to be someone who can deliver consistently over the long term. Gary points out, "You want to provide results that can be relied upon. This is not about having one good month, quarter, or year; you want to have consistent, continuous results over a tenure of 2, 3, or 4 years." **When you have consistent customer and employee interactions, you produce dependable results.**

In my career, I saw the effectiveness of consistency up close. A brilliant colleague named Jesse Washington was masterful at this. Recognizing the power that regular communication has in building trust, Jesse proactively set up regular check-ins with each of his customers. Though the frequency would vary depending on his customers' needs, his typical cadence was every two weeks. Jesse also made sure that these meetings were focused on his customers' needs and priorities, not his own need to hit a sales target. After asking his customer what topics would be of value for them, he coordinated with his extended team to have them join the calls to be on hand to solve specific challenges or drive discussions. After Jesse stepped up to the role of sales director, I reached out to one of the leading sales specialists on Jesse's new team, Mark Litwin. During our interview, I asked Mark about Jesse's consistency as a leader. Mark shared, "I can tell he is consistently thinking about the big picture. This shows in the way that he is always asking if you have everything you need to be successful. He is one of the best managers I have had." By keeping your focus on consistent communication and support, your customers and team will know you are someone they can trust.

Success Step

With customers and employees, establish a regular, predictable cadence for checking in. For customers, if you have access to a Customer Relationship Management (CRM) system, use it to set up triggers and reminders so that you will be notified when you haven't touched base with your customer or team in some time, or you have a response that is due to them. For those without a CRM system, create reminders in Outlook or Gmail calendars. Keep a list in Microsoft Excel or Google Sheets with each of your customers' contact info. In subsequent columns, write dates you last sent a message or talked with them on the phone. If you have various marketing campaigns that you run, I suggest you track that in something more suited for that purpose; however, using Excel or Sheets will work for those on a smaller budget.

For leaders, you may have more frequent, perhaps daily, interactions with your employees. Do not let daily communication lead you to think you have no need to schedule additional touchpoints. As most of your daily employee interactions focus on assigning new tasks and ensuring they are getting those tasks completed on time, these are not the type of interactions that will build the most trust. **Be sure to schedule consistent, structured time outside of the daily routines.** Use this time to talk about your employee's needs, challenges, and any new areas they would like to explore. Be sure there is no question or doubt in their minds that this time is about them and their needs, not your needs or the needs of the business.

Work closely with your customers and employees to find a communication schedule that they can rely on, then stick to it. **Consistent actions build consistent trust.**

Have Integrity in All That You Do

In the many interviews with leaders that I conducted for this book, one of the most common questions I asked was, "What traits are most important to be successful in sales or leadership?" With very few exceptions, the trait I heard most frequently was integrity. In fact, I found it interesting that many of the leaders I spoke to placed so much importance on integrity that they often assumed I was asking for something more profound or original. Of course, not all interviewees chose the word integrity itself, instead using words and phrases such as "authentic," "real," "sincere," "not fake," and "be who you say you are." Though you may initially interpret different meanings to these words, as you will read, they all speak to the need for integrity. **No matter what words these leaders used, it became clear that one of the most essential ways in which we build trust is through integrity**.

Acclaimed leadership speaker and author Brian Tracy said, "The glue that holds all relationships together, including the relationship between the leader and the led, is trust, and trust is based on integrity." In Invincible Principle 1, I shared that my clients and audiences frequently point to a used car salesperson as their top example of "a bad salesperson." They are not alone. Each year, Gallup conducts a survey that asks respondents to rate the "honesty and ethics" of various job fields. Year after year, including the most recent survey to date in 2018, car salespeople consistently ranked the 2nd-lowest field in perceived honesty (without much surprise, the lowest-ranked field was a politician).

The simple fact is that most of us associate used car sales with a lack of integrity. We feel a car salesperson is willing to do or say anything just to get us to buy something *now*! If there is an issue or defect with the car, we do not have confidence that the salesperson will tell us about it. This critical stereotyping of car salespeople does not even have to be based on a bad car-buying experience we have had ourselves. Any whiff of inauthentic behavior triggers a near-universal response of, "They came across like a used car salesman." This means that you must avoid any perception of dishonesty or lack of sincerity as you seek to build trust.

There are two aspects to having integrity—honesty and authenticity. First, we will answer the question of what it means to be honest with those we seek to serve. **Be honest in how you represent yourself and your organization. This means telling the truth, even uncomfortable truths.** Start by always telling the truth about what your products or services can do and *what they cannot*. If your product does not meet a particular customer requirement, be open and honest about it. Do not fall into the trap of landing a win if the win comes from not being honest about certain capabilities or your organization's ability to deliver on time. This is a win/lose scenario. Your short-term win came at your customer's and your integrity's expense. You may have gotten the sale or the new promotion, but you destroyed the trust. In the long run, you lose.

In sales scenarios, instead of just responding "No" when asked if your product or service can do something, this is your chance to dig deeper. Why are they asking about this feature or service? Is it something they are using today? What is the scenario they are trying to address? Not having this feature or service will affect how many people? There are many examples from my sales career where a customer asked about a feature that was not yet available at that time. The quick, honest response would have been "No." By taking the time to ask follow-up questions, I was often able to determine that it was not a feature that was currently available in the product they were using at the time, or it was only something a very small group of users had requested. Many times, by taking the time to understand how they intended to use the feature they were requesting, I was able to find a similar capability or workaround to address the problem. Ultimately, even if I had to admit that our product currently did not include the feature they were asking about, I was able to be honest about what our product could and could not currently do.

Honesty also means you must be willing to admit the truth about your own abilities. If your role requires certain skills or knowledge, either learn them or admit it is an area you are still developing. Your customers and team members do not expect you to know everything, so never make up an answer that you are not sure is correct. Instead, share that you need help from your extended team or your leadership to get the right answer. By showing your customers and employees that you will not say something you are not completely sure is accurate, you are showing your commitment to honesty, even when that honesty may be uncomfortable. You still are building trust by demonstrating you are someone of integrity.

The second component of integrity is authenticity. Authenticity means conducting yourself in a way that is true to who you are. We all have had experiences of spending a short amount of time with someone, then walking away with a sense that the other person was not being sincere. Do not let that be you. Instead, be yourself—appropriately. Let people get to know the real you. Are you quirky sometimes? Be quirky. Are you someone who has a playful side? Let them see it. Again, keep it professional and appropriate for the workplace, and of course, never be disrespectful to others. Let your customers, employees, and audiences see the real you. It's important!

Authenticity is also about being in the moment with your customers and employees. When learning about the importance of creating intentional connection, we reviewed the benefit of asking others about their needs and challenges. Being authentic encourages you to show a genuine interest in other people beyond their jobs. One way to do this is by challenging yourself each time you meet with them, find out something new and interesting. Is there something that you have in common? Do they have kids? If so, how old are the kids and what sports are they into? What did they do this past weekend? What hobbies do they have? Take a genuine interest in getting to know them.

We are trying to build trust. More accurately, we want others to trust us. Yet all of us have hypersensitive inauthenticity detectors. Others can sense when they are talking to the real you and when they are talking to someone who is pretending to be interested just to get something you want. To avoid this, simply lead, sell, speak, and live with integrity. **Let honesty and authenticity lead your actions and decision-making.** As Paula Liebergen, a senior director at Blue Prism told me, "The more human you are, the more you can relate to and care about other people, the more effective you're going to be as a leader." She went on to share something a former manager of hers instilled that still guides her today: "People don't care what you know until they know how much you care." **Your integrity will build trust and show you care.**

You Are Responsible

The final component in building trust is responsibility. **Having others feel confident and comfortable enough to trust us is our responsibility.** In sales roles, it does not matter whether you are the account executive or another member of the extended sales team, you are responsible for building trust. You must own your part of that responsibility. Are deliverables being completed on time? Is the customer getting all the information and follow-up that they requested? As a leader, are you exploring potential partners your team can utilize to serve clients better or pushing them to find good partners on their own? Can you proactively help shape organizational changes to ensure your team is more successful? As a speaker, are you learning to be comfortable setting up the technical components of your presentations or relying on others to know what to do? Taking responsibility for any element of the customer experience will make certain they are getting the best experience possible.

If something goes wrong, and it will, take responsibility. Customers and team members will feel more inclined to be patient and understanding if they feel you are owning the responsibility. Customers will never trust you if your response is, "It is out of my hands" or "That wasn't my fault because Bob was supposed to be looking into that for you." **Your customers want to know that you are always ready to take responsibility for their success.**

Of course, there are tasks for which you are *explicitly* responsible, those tasks that fall under your direct job description and established processes. I have little doubt that you are already a rock star when it comes to getting things done on time. Beyond that, I am suggesting that you grow your sense of *implicit* responsibility.

Do not assume another member of the team is going to get back to your customer with the answer to a question or with an important follow-up item that is needed to keep the project moving forward. Take responsibility for making sure it is being done. In smaller organizations, these lines of responsibility are typically clearer. When you are a sales team of just one or two people, you undoubtedly have more responsibility for the steps needed to delight your customers. As sales teams grow larger, I have found that team members often start losing that sense of implicit responsibility. They assume other members of the team are stepping up. This can lead to important tasks and communication slipping through the cracks when everyone assumes someone else has an item handled.

At first, some may resist this notion of taking on more implicit responsibility. How many of you want more responsibility? Anyone? No? Luckily, I am not suggesting that you must do everything yourself. After all, you have just as many balls in the air as your coworkers do. I am merely suggesting that you maintain a sense of responsibility beyond your immediate job description. Create a more collaborative environment where all members of the team feel a sense of shared responsibility and everyone works in tandem to serve the customer in the strongest way possible.

This same sense of responsibility can transform you from simply being a manager into being a leader. A manager gives orders, sets deadlines, and either rewards or disciplines employees when they finish tasks on time. A leader not only ensures that team members are working together to complete projects on time, but she also takes responsibility for understanding what they are going through as they do that work. Are there tools, systems, or training needed for your employees to better do their jobs? Hold yourself accountable for making sure your people are successful.

A leader must be willing to "get in the trenches" with her people. Dina Gallay, now the Vice President of Revenue at the global consulting firm RPG, described an example of this from when she was a new sales manager at LinkedIn: "When I first started, I could coach somebody on how to close business, but I didn't know some of their internal processes, such as using the Customer Relationship Management system. I realized quickly it was important for me to know what they experienced, so I asked my team to walk me through the CRM process from A to Z." By adopting a sense of responsibility, Dina took actions that quickly fostered trust from her employees.

A way of strengthening your connection with your customer, team, and audience is by asking for feedback on a frequent basis. Some of that will be very casual, "Did we meet your goal for this meeting?" or "Did we hit the mark today?" Some of this should be more structured, perhaps a monthly review. Ask them what they feel is going well and what is going... less well. "Am I exceeding your expectations, or what suggestions do you have that will make sure I exceed them next time?" This feedback loop also lends itself to Consistency. By asking for feedback, not only do you make sure you are staying aligned to the needs of those you serve, it also makes them feel valued. **Also, when it comes to feedback, though the asking is important, the *asking* means nothing without the *acting*.** Get the feedback, then take responsibility for making the appropriate adjustments that show you have heard and care about what was said.

The true power of responsibility is when a sense of implicit responsibility starts to drive explicit behaviors. **In all aspects of your life, you are response-*able*.** You are in control of how you respond to any event, situation, or feeling. As a speaker, you cannot control if the projector malfunctions during a key moment in your speech or if someone in the room interrupts you with a bizarre or negative comment. However, you can control your response to those events. Will you respond with frustration, impatience, or anxiety? Or will you respond with humor, patience, and confidence? Though you are not responsible for their actions, you are response-*able*.

Success Step

The world today is full of divisive politics, bullies, and anger-inducing news reports. Unless you are a divisive politician, bully, or maker of bad news, none of this is your responsibility. To all of it, you have a response-ability. Choose your response in a way that will help you keep moving forward. By doing so, those around you will respect you, look up to you, and importantly, come to trust you.

Challenge yourself to take responsibility (and response-ability) for everything that happens within your field of influence. Essentially, everything you see, do, or experience is within your field of influence. To ensure your success, try these two success steps. First, find a piece of paper (or sticky note) and write down the phrase, "I am responsible." Stick the note to your bathroom mirror, your monitor at work, or anywhere else you will see it frequently. Second, I encourage you to find a time each day to repeat "I am responsible" to yourself quietly. Find a few moments, free of distraction, to repeat that phrase to yourself. For me, I do it just before bed. I call it my "Response-able Moment." Just before falling asleep each night, I close my eyes and breathe in slowly several times. Then I repeat "I am response-able" at least two times, sometimes more. I encourage you to find your own Response-Able

Moment. Be intentional about it, making sure to do it every day, if not several times a day. Repeat "I am responsible." Feel how freeing it is, how empowering it is.

The world today is full of divisive politics, bullies, and anger-inducing news reports. Unless you are a divisive politician, bully, or maker of bad news, none of this is your responsibility. To all of it, you have a response-ability. Choose your response in a way that will help you keep moving forward. By doing so, those around you will respect you, look up to you, and importantly, come to trust you.

INVINCIBLE TIPS

1. Trust = Ability + Consistency + Integrity + Responsibility
2. Demonstrate your Ability by speaking up and sharing your knowledge with others
3. Have Consistency in your approach and cadence with your customers
4. Show your Integrity through honesty and authenticity
5. Be willing to take Responsibility for anything in your realm of control

SUMMARY

Trust is a foundational principle that is essential to our success. As sellers, leaders, and speakers, we will only be successful if we are trusted by those we are seeking to serve—a trust that will always be tough to gain, easily lost, and nearly impossible to gain back. **However, you can build trust in a predictable way by following the traits in the trust formula: T=A+C+I+R.** Those steps are the ongoing demonstration of your ability, the consistency in your communications and your approach, the integrity in all that you say and do, and the taking of responsibility for experiences and outcomes. By establishing trust in this way, others will open themselves to you. Not only that, it is through these four key traits that you continually shape the person that you want to be. A person others will come to know, like, and of course, *trust*.

INVINCIBLE PRINCIPLE 3: DEFINE A BOLD VISION

"Fortune befriends the bold."
— *Emily Dickinson*

Before we dive into the next principle, it is important to put these first few principles in perspective. Principles 1 and 2, (Create Intentional Connection and Build Lasting Trust), are foundational. They are the groundwork needed to be able to execute the remaining principles outlined in the coming chapters. However, though it is essential to become skilled at establishing connection and trust, being an expert in those two areas alone is not enough to stand out and excel in today's organizations. Instead, think of the first two Principles as what will get you in your customer's front door. They are what you need to earn the opportunity to serve. Only by mastering them will others be agreeable to share one of their most precious commodities, their time. However, the remaining principles are where you will truly stand out from others. **The energy put into mastering Principles 3-6 will not only determine the success of your sales, leadership, or speaking career, it will also determine the health and happiness of your entire life.**

By now, you have established the necessary foundation needed to serve your customer or team. You have taken your time, not rushing through these important first principles. You asked effective, practiced questions. You then used active listening and empathy to fully understand and feel their needs as if they were your own. This helps you recognize how those needs fit in the greater context of the team, department, company, etc. Now it is time for you to take the information that they have shared, along with the lasting trust that you have established, to serve in a way that only you can. The first way in which you demonstrate your unique contributions is through **Invincible Principle 3: Define a Bold Vision**.

Ask yourself these questions: What are the reasons to seek out products or services from other people or organizations? If you have ever had a coach, mentor, or worked with a consultant, what benefit did he or she provide? Why do you listen when a speaker or company leader is sharing information? Your answers are likely to vary. However, ultimately, most people's responses to these questions all share a common thread. **That common thread is that we buy products because we have a need that either we cannot fulfill ourselves or it is a poor use of our time to try to do so.**

We rarely go shopping when we perceive that we already have the best tools we need to do our jobs or to live our life effectively. An example of this would be the brilliant engineers at NASA. Undoubtedly, they could design and build a new line of SUVs. However, earth-bound automobile design does not align with their core mission. That is why when the good folks at NASA go on a road trip, they are driving SUVs from companies like Ford or GM just like the rest of us.

The same is true in leadership or coaching. When we feel we have all the knowledge and insights needed to do our jobs well and live our most Invincible life, we are far less inclined to seek help from others. During those moments of perceived low need, we rarely notice the unending marketing emails, commercials, and social media ads to which we are continuously subjected. We ignore products or insights that we perceive promise only a slight change or minor improvement to what we already have. We summarily dismiss those offers with a mental, "Why bother? I already have something that does most of those things." If there is any hope of catching our attention, the tool or insight must be a radical step up from what we already have, know, or do. With this simple understanding in mind, leaders, speakers, and sellers have a tremendous opportunity to separate themselves from what their peers or competitors may be offering.

Sales expert and founder of Seamless.AI, Brandon Bornancin reminds us to "solve a specific problem for a specific person in a specific niche." Those of us in sales and leadership must provide a unique offering or expertise that addresses our customer's unmet needs. To differentiate yourself, create an offering that is so game-changing, customers and employees cannot help but pay attention.

This is not a matter of creating a different offering than the one you currently have. Instead, create a *bold vision* that aligns your current offering to your customer's needs in a new and dynamic way. Let others play it safe. Let other sellers and leaders have small ideas that are just like everyone else in the industry. Instead, ensure those you serve understand how much better their workplace, careers, or lives can be. Provide clarity, focus, and the insights that will bring light to the places that are currently unlit in their minds. **When you help others discover the undiscovered, you help them see what they are not seeing for themselves.**

SEE WHAT THEY DO NOT SEE

Steve Jobs, Tony Robbins, Oprah Winfrey, and Richard Branson are just a few of the names we recognize as some of the world's most successful leaders. Each of them started her or his own businesses from scratch and then led those businesses to stratospheric success. Not surprisingly, not only are they great leaders, they have all been overwhelmingly successful in sales. Each of them has been responsible for producing billions of dollars in revenue. At the same time, they all enjoy tremendous success as speakers, inspiring millions to change their lives forever. Though these iconic individuals and others all have unique styles and skills, it would be hard to argue against the fact that each of them was especially brilliant at seeing opportunities and unmet needs that others did not see.

You, too, can see the paths, possibilities, and outcomes that others are not seeing. What can you provide for them that will not just make their jobs or lives easier but will be transformative to those you serve? What new streams of revenue can you unlock for them? What could they be doing differently that is not a consideration for them today? With your outside perspective, what areas of opportunity are they missing?

Your creative and unique answers to those questions and others like them will allow you to define your bold vision for those you serve. A great example of this came from Lee Brosnan, a healthcare sales executive who has worked at three of the largest service providers in the world. Lee recalled, "One of my most memorable career highlights was working with a hospital consortium. These are organizations that would normally compete with one another, yet we had a vision on how they could share information that would bring better care for the community. We saw ways in which they could improve population health, disease management, and more." Brosnan's team defined a bold vision of bringing multiple organizations together in new ways, creating a platform that has tremendously improved the standard of care in the community. This is what you can do when you allow yourself to see what others do not.

Vision is your opportunity to shine. **Your one-of-a-kind vision sets you apart from any other vendor, leader, or speaker.** Use your distinctive creativity and expertise when defining your vision. Allow yourself to be audacious and inspiring. Do not think small here. Do not play it safe. Embrace this chance to be a visionary. You must even be willing to let your vision scare you. Explore paths that will not always be easy but will result in something amazing. Bill Gagliard, a sales leader at Amazon Web Services, says that sellers and leaders "must be willing to jump into the ugly, the unknown. Take the worst job in the office. Because when it takes off, you have a launching pad to your success." What will your launching pad be?

 Success Step

To help you define your bold vision for your customer, the first step is to create a vision statement for those you serve. Just as every successful organization should define a vision statement at the organizational level, you must define a vision for your customer and team. This vision is your North Star, your guiding light. Without a clear vision of where you are going, how will you know if you get there? How will you recognize when your project or presentation is veering off track? And very importantly, as we will soon learn, it will be difficult to inspire others to follow you if you are not crystal clear as to where you would like to go. Just because you have established some connection and trust does not mean that others will follow you blindly. **By taking the time to set a clear vision, you significantly improve the likelihood that your customers and team will be willing to go on the journey with you.**

To get started with your vision for your customer, think one year into the future. What does success look like for your team, your customer, or those you hope to serve? One year from now, when your vision is realized (and it will be), what will have happened? Write the expected outcomes down on paper or your favorite electronic notes app. A vision is future-facing, so keep it centered on *what* you will make happen for your customer, not the *how*. Add as many outcome-focused details as you know today. The more specific and detailed it is, the more clarity your vision will provide you.

Start with whatever comes to mind right now, then add more detail over time. The most successful individuals will have 1-year, 3-year, and 5-year customer vision plans. Having a clear vision is not only essential in determining what value you have to offer others, it will allow you to assemble the right team to execute on that vision. A strong vision will help you persist when you face setbacks and surprises. In other words, **a clear vision does not just help you prepare for the future, it will help you get there.**

Your vision statement for those you serve should be just as bold as some of the leading corporate visions.

Some examples include:
- "To serve as the most trusted leader in investment services." – Charles Schwab
- "To radically shift the global economy toward life-fulfilling independent ventures." – GoDaddy
- "Realizing the full potential of the internet to drive a new era of development, growth, and productivity." – Creative Commons
- "To offer designer eyewear at a revolutionary price, while leading the way for socially conscious businesses." – Warby Parker
- "Empower every person and every organization on the planet to achieve more." – Microsoft
- "To be the company that best understands and satisfies the product, service and self-fulfillment needs of women—globally." – Avon
- "To become the world's most loved, most flown, and most profitable airline." – Southwest Air

As I noted, those were corporate vision statements. **Your customer vision statement should exude the same confident tone.** Make a declaration. As a speaker, imagine yourself standing in front of a group of people who are leaders at a small regional airline. They have asked you to speak to them on how to create growth in new markets. Imagine yourself starting the presentation by saying, "Today, I will share with you some ideas on how to expand your business." Perhaps they will pay attention, or perhaps they will quickly be checking their phones. What if, instead, you defined a bold vision for your program, such as, "Over the next sixty minutes, I will share with you the steps needed to become the world's most loved, most flown, and most profitable airline." Every leader in that room will be ready to listen to what you have to say.

This exercise may seem very similar to the Invincible goal-setting exercise we did in Chapter 1. As I encouraged you to set a vision of what success would look like for you, we are now going through the same process for those you serve. Become great at crafting and maintaining vision statements for both yourself and your customer. When you do, you will always be growing together.

Remember, do not limit yourself to stating only something you know *how* to deliver. A vision statement is not about *how*, it is about *what*. What will your team, audience, or customer have achieved 1-2 years from now because of the services you provide? What bold outcome have they realized? **Your vision is not a plan. Your vision is the reason a plan will be made.**

Differentiate Through Value

A short time ago I discovered the truth about diamonds. For all of you diamond-lovers out there, you may want to sit down. Of course, we all know that diamonds are considered a precious gem, a distinction they share with other gems like ruby, sapphire, and emerald. If you gave a loved one a ruby, sapphire, or emerald for her birthday, anniversary, or other noteworthy days, I suspect she would be excited and very appreciative. However, when it comes to those truly special occasions such as an engagement, wedding, or grand expression of love, only a diamond will do. Imagine my surprise when I recently learned that diamonds are so valuable largely because of good old-fashioned capitalism.

Diamonds have become valuable simply because many years ago one company bought up most of the world's supply, then did some very smart marketing. This created a surge in demand. The growth in demand resulted in higher prices, which in turn increased the perceived value of diamonds far above other gems.

That sort of gamesmanship in supply and demand is not overly uncommon or noteworthy. Yet, when it comes to diamonds, there is an unexpected twist.

Beginning in the 1950s, scientists and gemologists began manufacturing synthetic diamonds by super-heating carbon crystals. On a molecular level, these lab-grown diamonds are almost identical to natural diamonds mined from the earth, making manufactured diamonds nearly as strong. In addition, the human eye is incapable of seeing any difference between a lab-grown diamond and those found naturally.

The starkest contrast comes in the cost of production. Lab-grown diamonds are produced for significantly less cost than mining, without any of the ethical concerns that hang over a natural diamond's origin. Yet, thanks to more smart marketing by natural diamond suppliers, despite the same quality, same beauty, and lower cost, these lab-grown diamonds have only a fraction of the perceived value of their earth-mined twins.

Which brings us to the challenge of value. How do you define it? If I told you that I was going to give you a gift of a pink unicorn named Polly, am I providing value to you? No? Perhaps not you, but the person sitting next to you at the office might feel ecstatic to have a pink unicorn named Polly. He would tell everyone he knows, proudly showing off pictures of Polly any chance he got. For him, Polly's value would be priceless. A real-world example of this came from one of my wife's coworkers. "Susan" had a purebred Pomeranian dog. She doted over that dog, talking to my wife about her fabulous companion nearly every day. When the dog unexpectedly died, within a few weeks, "Susan" paid $5,000 for another Pomeranian. She was perfectly willing to do so because of the value she placed on that particular breed. At the same time, my wife and I are quite certain that if they were in a "Best Dog" competition against one another, our $200 mixed-breed rescue dog would put that little Pom to shame. Yes, we are a little biased about our dog. But that is the thing about value: it is perceived and personal. **Value, like beauty, is in the eye of the beholder.**

That presents a challenge for those of us who earn a living by providing value to others. A question my clients frequently ask is, "If value is personal and may change over time, how will I know if my offering will actually be of value to the other person?" To get those you are trying to serve to understand the value of what you have to the point they are ready to invest in it, two factors must align.

First, be certain your product or service has value to the person you are targeting. You may have created the greatest product in the history of the world, but if it is not something your customer is seeking, you are wasting your time. Go spend your energy with another customer who will better appreciate your product. This is especially true in sales because if your customer does not see the value, he or she will ask you for incentives or price reductions. Avoid the need to offer discounts by targeting those who have an immediate need for your offering.

The second dynamic of value is what you can provide beyond the offering itself. This is where you have the greatest opportunity to differentiate yourself from others. **This is where your knowledge of your customer and your creativity really comes into play.** Your offering has value, yet you are not alone in the marketplace. Chances are, there are other companies or individuals who provide a product or service with many of the same features and functionality, at largely the same price. In some industries, such as technology, retail, healthcare, and others, there are often many choices for your customer. In leadership, right within your own organization, there are other leaders serving the needs of their team and the business, just like you are. To differentiate yourself, you need to explore fully the ways in which you can provide value that others are not. Just as we discovered in setting a bold vision, find differentiated solutions and services by being creative and focused on your customer's needs.

Put yourself in the shoes of those you are trying to serve. Doug Ennis, Vice President of Sales for NS1, told me, "For us, the process of providing value starts on day one. As we're just getting our foot in the door with a new customer, we're already thinking about value.

This often starts with doing the research to understand their specific industry. But most importantly, aligning that with what they are telling you regarding their needs." When creating intentional connection, as you did in Principle 1, what did your customer or team member tell you was their greatest need? What were their pain points? If needed, go back and ask specific questions that will help you identify where they perceive the value to be.

Questions such as:
1. What is it about your current solution that is the most/least valuable?
2. Are there things your current vendor is doing that is more/less valuable?
3. Beyond pricing, how do we exceed expectations in terms of value?
4. How much value does (insert your idea here)? Is there a way that could be made more valuable?
5. As a team member, what is it about past leaders that was more/less valuable?
6. What are the types of things I can do to make you feel more valued as a customer/employee?

With the answers to these value questions in hand, it is time to look at your offerings, expertise, and network from their perspective. Get super creative. What can be done that will be distinctive? Is there additional training you can make available to ensure their success with your service? Can recurring appointments be set up with them and key members of your team to answer any questions they have in the first month of using your product? Are there whitepapers, walkthroughs, or conversations with other customers that can be arranged to help them feel more comfortable in making a transition to your offering? As a leader, beyond business reviews, do you provide monthly coaching sessions? Can you introduce your team members into other parts of your organization where they may have some interests? Find creative solutions that add value to your leadership.

Yes, value is specific to the customer you seek to serve. To some, this could be a challenge to know what is unique, compelling, and effective. **To you, this is another opportunity to use creativity and connection to home in on finding the perfect value that ignites a fire in those you serve.**

THE STRENGTH OF YOUR TEAM

Before I moved into my corporate career, I was a professional speaker working for a private seminar company based in Miami. Each day, I would travel by plane to a new location in North America. Each night, I would deliver a 3-hour presentation focused on improving health and the quality of life for all in attendance. The pressure was high, the travel exhausting, and the amount of work was daunting. It was also one of the most rewarding jobs in my life.

That sense of pride and satisfaction came not just from the sheer number of people whose lives we touched; it was also the first time I recall becoming aware of the incredible, Invincible power of a professional team. From the marketing, event planning, and administrative support teams back in the home office, to the skilled hotel and venue staff that never stopped hustling to make sure the rooms were set up properly, to the on-site teams sent by placement agencies to handle everything from attendee registration to merchandise sales. Every night, this team of 20-30 individuals, most of us strangers to each other when we started the day, would all come together to create an experience for participants that very well could change their lives. That is what is possible from the strength of your team.

Very few in business would argue the importance of team. Not too many years ago, a team was a defined group of people, clustered together in cubicles, all sharing the same physical office. The group members largely shared information only with other members of that same group. That was easy to do because if you had a question or wanted assistance from another team member, you only needed to walk a few feet away to have that conversation.

Today, that outdated paradigm is nearly extinct. Organizations ranging from small businesses to the largest enterprises no longer think of a team as being limited to the same set of people in a shared physical space. Using resources such as open or shared officing, plus growing support for team members who work from home, businesses now have tremendous flexibility on who can work together at any given time and on any given project. Add to that, technologies such as video conferencing and collaboration apps enable any business to pull together individuals from separate teams or separate organizations, making it common for team members to be across the country or around the world.

These advances in technology and work environments provide an opportunity to reshape teams to fit our needs to create the best experience for our customers. With the speed of change happening today, it is impossible for us to know or do everything ourselves as we work to serve others. Most of us, from solopreneurs to global firms, depend on others to provide a higher level of service to our customers.

Given the complexity and competition today, effective teaming is essential to success in sales. Mike Rocco, the CEO of 3Cloud says, "The concept of being a lone hunter is outdated and ineffective. Businesses change too quickly. The only way to address that is by coming at it as a team." Another top leader, Ross Friedman, the CEO of Rightpoint, reinforced this reality when discussing a top challenge today. He tells us, "Today, it is almost impossible for a seller to sell by themselves. They must have a team to be able to define and articulate the full scope of what's possible."

Steps to building a strong team:
1. Choose the right people
2. Define and delegate
3. Encourage creativity
4. Monitor progress while celebrating success

1. Choose the right people – Explore working with teams outside of the usual groups you tend to work with today. Do not allow organizational silos to stop the formation of new team partnerships aimed at bringing a better outcome for those you serve. When determining individuals to add, consider not only what skills each member brings to the team, but how those contributors work best. Some members of the team will thrive through close collaboration and frequent touchpoints, while others will excel if they are given space to work independently without distraction. Both work styles can create outstanding results when you take the time to understand and best support them.

    2. **Define and Delegate** – Clearly defining what success will look like keeps the team focused and marching toward the common goal. Communicate the benefit the team will provide and how their work fits into the overall needs of the customer. Your vision statement will be extremely useful here. Patrick Rams of Capgemini says, "Articulate the mission and the why of what you are doing." Use delegation while promoting routine information-sharing. This avoids duplication of effort while adding the security of multiple team members being capable of filling in for one another during critical times.

    3. **Encourage Creativity** – Your customers need innovative and creative ideas! Give group members the latitude to try radical and refreshing approaches to the challenges your customers face. Your competitors will look bland and behind-the-times as you offer new streams of revenue or solutions your customer does not currently have in place. Plan brainstorming sessions without being limited to only those ideas the group knows _how_ to make happen. Innovation ignores the how!

    4. **Monitor progress while celebrating success** – Establish a predictable cadence for status updates, respecting the work styles of group members and any deadlines and dependencies. Use update calls to understand how you can best assist the team's efforts. Create an atmosphere in which members are recognized for both helping each other and asking for help. Make team members feel their contributions are important and valued while celebrating innovative thinking and task completion. You win together!

To succeed in sales and leadership today requires the strength of a team. Bringing the right individuals together amplifies their collective skills to produce new ideas and solutions. Keep your team focused on delivering on the bold vision as you recognize contribution and success.

The right team, aligned behind a bold vision, can create truly exceptional results.

Invincible Tips

1. A bold vision sets you apart from others
2. Value must be aligned to the customer's immediate needs
3. Use value to differentiate yourself in ways your competition cannot
4. Assemble your team carefully, then trust in their ability
5. Encourage all team members to contribute creatively

Summary

Your customers and team members have unmet needs. Because of those needs, you can serve them by helping them to see solutions they do not currently see. Do this by defining a bold vision, moving away from the competition or status quo. Do not be limited to only that which you currently know how to achieve. Instead, be a visionary. Push beyond incremental improvements for those you serve. Start by writing out a clear, audacious vision statement for your customers or employees. Next, reinforce that statement by adding value based on their needs. Make your offering irresistible by exploring interesting partnerships or deliverables that will pack even more value into your vision. Finally, assemble the best team and give them the freedom to work together to deliver the vision. As they progress, recognize their efforts and bold thinking. **Remember, when you help others to discover the undiscovered, you help them see what they are not seeing for themselves.**

INVINCIBLE PRINCIPLE 4: SPEAK WITH IMPACT

"Your number one mission as a speaker is to take something that matters deeply to you and rebuild it inside the mind of your listeners."
— Chris Anderson

Last fall, I had the pleasure of working with Tammy, the CEO of a mid-sized services organization. As CEO, Tammy is continuously speaking to both internal and external audiences. The nature of the presentations and audiences can vary on any given occasion, from executive team events to customers envisioning conversations to large keynote speeches in front of hundreds of people. When we first started working together, she shared with me that while speaking to others, she feels confident, knowledgeable about the organization, and articulate. However, she did not always feel her message resonated with the audience, and because of that, she was not getting the results she wanted.

Tammy had a large keynote speech coming up at an industry trade show where hundreds of people would be in attendance, including many executives, plus current and potential customers. She knew what was at stake. This speech would be one of her most important of the year, making it essential that her message connected with those in attendance and inspired them to act.

Tammy and I did not have much time before her big speech. Fortunately, we were able to utilize the "Speak with Impact" system I developed for my clients. This gave her a better understanding of areas where her speech and delivery could be improved. This included providing more clarity and structure to the content, weaving a central message throughout the speech, and injecting moments of humor to build rapport with the audience. Since no speech is complete without stories, we identified several relevant ones to emphasize key moments. Finally, we spent time on Tammy's stage work, making sure her movements were purposeful and planned. She was now ready for her big night.

The morning after the speech, Tammy called me. Her energy was palpable. I could feel her glowing through the phone. "It was amazing!" she exclaimed. "I have never felt that confident on stage. The audience was with me the whole time. It was so much fun!" She then told me that in addition to the many compliments she got afterward, executives from two different organizations approached her. They both shared that they were so inspired by her message that they wanted to set up meetings with her team to understand better how her company could help them create the future outcome she had described. I later learned that several other potential customers had also arranged for meetings with Tammy's sales teams. Not only had she inspired those in attendance, but she had also uncovered multiple sales opportunities, all while thoroughly enjoying herself. **That is the power of speaking with impact,** which leads us to **Invincible Principle 4: Speak with Impact**.

I left the corporate world to create my own business because I recognized that salespeople and leaders must make the most out of every moment they have when speaking in front of others. For my clients, those moments can include customer presentations, sales or investor pitches, leadership reviews, talking to a customer in their office, and many more. Do you speak in front of others? If you are in sales, leadership, entrepreneurship, or most any profession, the answer to that question is a resounding "Yes!"

Chances are, with the dynamic changes happening in the world today, you likely find yourself jumping from one video call to another. You may also be using video platforms to lead team meetings, conduct internal training sessions, public webinars, or even sharing content about your organization on social media. **Regardless of whether you are in the same room with your audience or speaking to others around the world, there are universal elements you should be using to make sure your message is connecting with your audience and motivating them to act on that message.**

I developed my "Speak with Impact" system to help anyone looking to communicate more effectively. These are the same communication techniques I used to prepare for the 1500+ sales and leadership presentations that I delivered during my corporate career. I now use these techniques in my own business, including while I prepared for my TEDx Talk in the fall of 2019. **This system has now become the most sought-after content in my consulting and speaking business, helping sales teams and leaders achieve higher sales and better employee engagement.** Using this system to prepare for your next presentation, speech, or sales call will give you greater confidence, purpose, and results.

Research continues to show that the average attention span is dropping at an alarming pace. Microsoft Research conducted a study in 2015 (about.ads.microsoft.com/en-us/insights/stories/intelligent-connections), which showed that the average attention span had shortened to just 8 seconds! **8 SECONDS!** Thanks to the widespread use of social media, this shortening trend is accelerating globally, as shown by a study out of Europe in April 2019 (eurekalert.org/pub_releases/2019-04/tuod-aoi041119.php). However, do not panic or give up hope just yet. **There are things you can do to be effective every time.**

A Strong Opening

Whether your goal is to inform, inspire, or motivate, there are key elements that you can use to make certain that you are fully resonating with your audience. **Those four elements are a strong opening, a clear solution, great stories, and a compelling close.**

What entails a strong opening? Let's first understand what a strong opening is **not**. Have you ever sat through a sales presentation, lecture, or informational seminar where the speaker spends the first 3-5 minutes talking about *himself*? He goes on and on about his credentials, the credentials of the company he represents, or a detailed explanation of his job history? "For over fifty years, Agency X has been a leader in subprime investment portfolio management while winning more Purple Hippo Awards than... blah, blah, blah." If this is how you open your presentations and pitches, I have some unfortunate news that you must be prepared to accept–No one cares.

Sure, of course, they want you to have done something of note at some point before today, but the people who care enough to want your detailed background will have likely already looked you up on social media or studied your company's website. Skip the boring recitation of your work history. Instead, make the most of those first few minutes of the meeting. Do that by grabbing their attention and then setting a clear outcome.

Use those first moments to engage the audience right away. Find a way to make them think. Get them immediately interested and thinking that this is not going to be just another long, boring sales pitch or lecture that they must suffer through. Be different from any other speaker by being *interesting* and *interested* in their needs. There are several ways to do this. My favorites include asking a few purposeful questions, telling a brief story, or by saying something intriguing.

By asking questions, I am not suggesting a repeat of the questions you asked back in Principle 1 (Create Intentional Connection).

Instead, use questions that are meant to draw the audience into the talk by being relatable to most people in attendance or questions that will likely get a large majority to raise their hands and engage.

Some examples are:

- Can anyone share a moment when… ?
- Have you noticed that recently… ?
- How many have ever experienced… ?
- When was the last time you… ?
- Have you ever wished that 'XX' was less complicated?

With smaller groups, ask people to share short responses. As they do, repeat back what the person said in a way that acknowledges their contribution. Thank them for sharing and then move on to others in order to get more people engaged. In larger groups, you may choose either to take responses from a small number of people or ask those in attendance to raise their hand if they agree or disagree with a statement you have made. When many people raise their hand, point to someone and ask, "Will you share why you agree with what I just said?" This type of immediate interaction leads to the audience paying closer attention, telling themselves they must be ready in case you call on them. I am not above causing a little friendly anxiety if it keeps people's attention!

To use questions effectively, I suggest these tips. First, be careful of the overuse of questions that seem gimmicky. When addressing a room full of executives, asking "How many of you like ice cream?" will likely be met with impatient scowls. Also, avoid asking questions that make the audience look foolish or unknowledgeable. This is never a good idea. A question such as "Who can tell me how many plastic straws Americans use each month?" may seem interesting, but if response after response has you saying to those responding, "No, that's not right. Who else has a guess?" it is time to use a different question. It is more effective for you to reframe the same question by saying "Raise your hand if you think the number of straws used per day is more than five hundred thousand." Your point is still made, without making the audience look uninformed.

The next option to create a strong opening is to tell a brief story. We will go into detail on stories in the next chapter; however, there is an important difference between a story that you may use to begin your presentation or speech and the stories you will be utilizing in the next chapter. The primary difference between an opening story and other stories you may use is the length. Most often, opening stories are 30-60 seconds long. Stories you will include later in your presentation can be longer, though most stories will typically not be longer than a few minutes. As with all things, this is not a hard and fast rule. No one is timing the length of the opening story, ready to sound a buzzer if it goes past a minute. Just keep in mind those opening moments are meant to grab attention, so either brevity or great storytelling is the key.

Another strong opening is to say something intentionally provocative or intriguing. This is very effective to get the customer or audience thinking. If you are a fan of TEDx Talks, a great opening moment that highlights the use of intrigue is Daniel Pink's popular talk entitled "The Puzzle of Motivation." In the first moment, he shares, "I need to make a confession. A little over twenty years ago, I did something I regret." As a listener, I am immediately intrigued by what he may reveal. He continues: "In a moment of youthful indiscretion, I went to law school." It is a great surprise. Your example of intrigue can be just as simple. Instead of saying, "Good morning, how is everyone doing today? Thank you for your time. I am excited to be here..." (yawn), imagine if you stepped up and said, "We knew we were going to be able to help our customer, but even we were shocked two months later when the CEO told us something that we never expected. Do you want to know what she said? I cannot wait to tell you... in just a few minutes." Everyone loves a secret. If you try that with your audience, I promise they will be paying attention.

After the strong opening, it is time to set the main message for your talk. You need one distinct statement of what your talk is all about. **This main message is what you want them to remember, even if they remember nothing else.** Your main message is essentially telling the audience what the outcome of your presentation will be. When the presentation is over, what will the audience have gotten from it? How will they be thinking differently? As the goal for any meeting, discussion, or presentation is to inform, inspire, and lead the audience to think differently than they do today, the main message is stating right up front what this new way of thinking will be. In the example of a sales pitch, the goal is to enable the customer to see your offering differently or more clearly. There is also another benefit to having the main message. By sharing the outcome for your presentation upfront, your audience knows how to organize and retain the information they will hear. They have the context right from the start. As they hear more details, the listener remembers those details better because they are now connected in their minds.

The main message for your talk should be clear, concise, and compelling. Ideally, the main message is constructed from those questions you asked and the great listening you did while building connection and trust in Principles 1 and 2. Aligning the presentation to your customer's needs will show her that you are here to better serve her organization. We all have seen many presentations in our careers that have had little to no impact. Make sure your customer or audience member knows right up front that you have something of value to offer that aligns with her needs.

Do not undersell the value you provide with a weak main message. This means avoiding the use of vague words like "improve" or "help." Do you want to sit through a sales pitch that has the goal to "help you improve your production capacity while you lower costs?" Not unless it includes a free lunch. Be **BOLD**! For example, proudly say, "We are here today to double your sales in the next two years while creating radical delight for your customers." Another example, "Today, we will unlock the hidden insights in your patient data, enabling you to transform care while saving lives." A leadership example would be, "This program is designed to cultivate and reward standout team members while empowering every employee to build a career they love." These statements are clear, they are bold, and they are based on the needs of those with whom you are speaking.

A strong opening starts by grabbing the audience's attention and setting a clear outcome for the discussion. When you do that, those you serve are ready to listen.

A Clear Solution

Now that you have the attention of your customer or intended audience and you have defined the outcome-based main message, it's time to get down to the business of laying out your solution. Here is where the rubber meets the road. **How are you and your organization specifically going to solve their challenges?** What makes you different from other competitors or leaders? How are you going to produce the outcome you stated in your main message? What are the steps involved? What examples do you have from previous customers that will help the audience feel confident in your offering? All these questions and more can be addressed as you lay out the solution.

Unfortunately, as the solution is the bulk of your content, too often, **it is also the area where the bulk of mistakes happen for the speaker.** If it is any consolation, this issue is not your fault. This is how you were taught to present without even being aware of it. As we grow up and go through school, day after day, we are exposed to countless lackluster lectures delivered by uninspired speakers. This is in no way intended to bash the many wonderful educators out there. Almost every one of us has had the good fortune to have our lives touched in some way by an inspired and inspiring teacher. Yet for every elementary teacher through tenured college professor who genuinely shapes their students' lives, there are others who haphazardly recite facts to a room full of captive pupils. Students pay attention for no more reason than their grades depend on it. As a result, after several decades of schooling, without even realizing it, most of us have come to accept two factors that are working to spoil future presentations.

First, as a listener, we come out of the schooling system thinking something akin to, "If I ever have to listen to another lecture in my life, I swear I am going to jump off a bridge." This causes most of us to avoid both sitting through and giving presentations at all costs. At the same time, after years of bad examples, we have been unwittingly trained that a speaker's job is to recite a long list of facts and nothing more. As wave after wave of former students take their places in the workforce, with no training on how effective speaking and presenting _should_ be done, the same two issues now spread into the working world. When we do see a trained speaker, we bestow upon her some inexplicable gift for presentation greatness. "She is a natural. I could never do that." The cycle spins on.

The full "Speak with Impact" system is a comprehensive program designed to remedy most issues that come up when presenting or speaking to others. In this book, we will walk through some of the most common issues and how they can be remedied. **I am happy to share that the most common problems that happen during the solution portion of your speech can be easily fixed.**

Let's start with the most common challenge: confidence. One of the fastest ways to give yourself confidence is to remind yourself before any presentation or speaking opportunity that you are there to serve. You are there to address the needs of your customer. This reminder alone keeps the focus off of you and on your customer, which helps boost confidence. As you grow more proficient in the remaining common challenges, your confidence will soar.

Another common issue is connecting to those in attendance. This can be accomplished in several ways. As I mentioned above, a good speaker approaches a talk or presentation by seeing it as an opportunity to get that audience to think differently. To do this, think of your presentations in terms of a journey. A journey from where they are today (with a challenge or need) to where they could be (using your solution). As with any journey, moving your customers or team members to this new place needs to start where they are today. Relate your solution to their needs throughout your talk. This level of personalization of your talk not only greatly improves the likelihood those listening will think differently because of the solution you lay out for them, but it will also help to keep their interest because it shows you understand their organization and current situation.

One of the easiest and surprisingly powerful ways to connect with your audience while speaking is by using their first names. A recent guest on my podcast, speaker and communication skills expert Lynne Franklin describes why this is so effective. She explains, "To each of us, the most important word in the English language is our name." Find moments to reference customers by name in an authentic manner. This immediately catches the attention of most everyone in the room, regardless of whether it was their name. Try it out during your next presentation.

 Success Step

Make a "Names Cheat Sheet" for yourself. As I was always notoriously bad at remembering names of people I had just met, I got into the habit of keeping a small piece of paper with me while attending customer or internal meetings. As people in the room introduce themselves, I write the name down in the configuration of where they are sitting in the room. Then when I speak, I take quick glances at the paper and make it a point to refer to several people by name. For example, "Earlier, Sandra told us one of her challenges is looking for a way to better collaborate with other teams," or "Imagine if Franco had a flat tire and he had never changed one before." This small gesture, if used authentically, has effective results.

Another common mistake made while laying out the solution is lack of clarity. To do this well, use 3-5 clearly defined data points that support your main message and align them to their needs. Think of each supporting data point as building on the one before. Referencing back to the idea of a journey, in the solution section of your presentation, you are methodically moving the customer through the journey, step by step. Be sure he is understanding each point clearly along the way. For even more clarity, use repetition to reinforce each of the data points. One way I like to do this is with a method I describe as, "Tell them what you are going to tell them, tell them, then tell them what you just told them." To use this method, after your strong opening, tell the audience what supporting points you are about to cover. Then, move through the points, one by one, handling questions after each supporting point. When finished with the last point of your solution, very briefly recap all of the data points that you walked through. By using this method to describe your solution details, it improves memory retention and gives you many more opportunities to interact with your customer.

Speaking of interaction, another common issue when speaking is assuming your customer is still with you on the journey. Just because he has not walked out of the room does not mean he is still with you. The only way to know for sure is to ask. Bad presenters do all the talking for an hour before finishing with, "That was everything I wanted to cover. Any questions?" Okay presenters will pause occasionally throughout their presentations and ask, "Any questions?" Confident, experienced presenters will pause at the end of each point and ask, "Is this content in line with your expectations for today?" or "Was that point clear? Would this solution area be useful for your organization?" By frequently checking with your audience, you will quickly know whether they are still with you or if adjustments are needed. The sooner you make the adjustments, the more aligned your solution will be.

This brings us to an area where *many* egregious mistakes happen—your slides. Far too many presenters have a clear misunderstanding of the role that slides have in a presentation. This may be difficult to hear, but it is best if we get this out of the way: **If you are a speaker who depends on your slides, *you are doing it wrong*.** Disagree all you want, but the truth is still the truth. I am not saying you are not allowed to use slides. On the contrary. I have used thousands of slides in my presentations. (Thankfully, not all at the same time!) What I am saying is, anyone who relies on slides is misusing them. Slides and visuals should be used to support you, not do your job for you.

The most common mistake when using slides is far too much content on the slides themselves. Uncomfortable presenters fill the slides with endless bullets points containing near-complete sentences in each bullet. This mistake invites the audience to read the information rather than listen to what you are saying. If you feel those watching must be able to read and listen at the same time, you are quite mistaken. It turns out, what we think of as multitasking is actually not possible. When your customer or audience member is trying to read the slides and listen to you speak, he or she will not do either one well. The more someone reads, the more your voice fades from their attention. Improve comprehension by making sure the slides only have a few bullet points per page and no more than six words per bullet. **Keep your audience focused on your speaking, not the slides.**

Because your solution is the heart of your presentation, pitch, or discussion, it can also be an area that is filled with common issues. Find several opportunities throughout your talk to connect your solution to their needs. Use a well-defined structure to keep your points clear, repetition to be remembered, and simple slides to keep the focus on what you are saying. By doing this, you take your customer along a journey to a new way of thinking and to the point where he or she is ready to take action!

The Compelling Close

Though this is far from scientific fact, based on my own experience, I am quite certain that 99% of meetings and presentations end poorly. As we have covered, unskilled presenters tend to rattle through their content and then briskly end with, "Any questions?" Oftentimes this is a sign that a nervous presenter is desperately hoping there will be no questions so that he can quickly move away from the front of the room. Even confident, skilled presenters who interact and engage their audiences throughout the presentation often end the meeting in a whimper. She makes the mistake of wrapping up the last point of their solution, asking for any last questions, then says "Well, that's all I have. Thank you for your time." In doing so, she misses one of the most important elements in speaking with impact: the compelling close.

Just as with your strong opening, there are two elements to your compelling close. The first element is your Call to Action. You are likely already familiar with the term Call to Action or CTA. What do you want your customer or team member to do next? No presentation, and I would argue no meeting, should end without clearly articulating what you would like your audience to do next. How should they take action based on the solution you just shared? They are never more likely than at this moment to take the action you are directing them to take. Do not miss this moment!

If this is a sales presentation, it may be time to ask for the sale. If this meeting is early in the sales process, perhaps the right next step is for them to start a small pilot to try your offering for themselves. At the very least, get them to schedule the next meeting within the next two weeks so you can do a demonstration or detailed walk-through of your product or service offerings. Even if your primary purpose is not to sell but to inform your customer about something she or he may already own, I still encourage you to include a CTA. Ask for another meeting to discuss how they can use these new capabilities, which gives you another chance to serve. Whatever the right next step may be, ask for that commitment in your CTA.

For leaders, your CTA to team members could be for them to write down two stretch goals they will commit to for the year ahead before they leave the meeting, or for them to agree to contact four additional prospects a day through the end of the sales year. Perhaps you want them to contact two people outside of your team and ask them to be their mentor. If you are speaking to an outside group, you may want the audience to visit your website for a free download or connect with you on social media. Again, whatever the appropriate action may be, make sure it aligns with the presentation's main message and the solution you provided as well as, most importantly, the challenges with which your audience struggles.

To increase the chances the audience will respond to your CTA, make it simple for them by narrowing the CTA down to one clear task. What is the one thing you need them to do? Last year, I was working with an enterprise sales team who insisted, "One CTA will never work. We need to give our customers several actions they can take." They started to roll through all the various follow-up actions a customer could take after their presentations. I clarified, "Deciding what action to take next is ultimately up to your customer but listing all these possibilities will only confuse them and make it less likely they decide on any of them." As an alternative, I suggested they use the CTA to give their customer only two possible follow-up actions, then finish with, "Given these two options, which one would you like to move forward with today?" **Several months later, the team shared that their customer follow-up rate was up by over 30%.**

The other element in a compelling close is what I call "The Button." "The Button" is the final 30-60 seconds of your presentation or meeting. After having answered all of their questions and stated your Call to Action, it is time to bring your presentation to a satisfying close. The Button serves as a summary and an opportunity to reiterate your vision once again. Because of that, put some thought into the final words that you are going to leave with your audience. Typically, I will coach my clients to "bookend" the speech by referencing back to something they said in those opening few moments. Ideally, your solution has delivered on the promise of that opening main message, so refer back to it in those final moments.

An example may be, "When I started speaking today, I shared that our goal is to double your sales in the next six months while creating radical customer delight. By partnering with us to implement the services designed to fit your needs, I feel confident that doubling your sales is just the beginning. With your well-establish leadership, you are poised to create an experience for your customers unlike any other." This type of button brings the entire presentation full circle, making it clear to your customer that you have met the goal you defined for the meeting.

A compelling close ensures your audience is ready to act.

Invincible Tips

1. No matter the situation, use the universal elements to effective speaking
2. Use the first moments of your speech or presentation to grab your audience's attention
3. Share the main idea that is clear, concise, and compelling
4. Always make sure your solution is tied to your audience's needs
5. End your talk with a clear call to action

Summary

Any time you present in front of those you serve, you have an incredible opportunity to move them to think differently and take action. Build on the connection, trust, and vision that you have established by making certain your powerful message resonates with those you serve. Whether your intent is to sell, educate, inform, or inspire, this simple system will move your customer, team members, or audience through a journey from where they are today to what is possible for them in the future. You can avoid common pitfalls and overcome years of bad presentation role models by using techniques that improve clarity and connection. Catch and keep their attention with a strong opening. Keep the focus on your audience using structure and interaction as you lay out your clear solution. Finally, motivate your audience to act by giving a clear call to action. By following these steps, along with adding the great stories that you will learn in the next chapter, you will always Speak with Impact.

INVINCIBLE PRINCIPLE 5: SHARE GREAT STORIES

"Storytelling is about connecting to other people and helping people see what you see."
— Michael Margolis

In late February of 2020, I was asked to do a keynote speech at the Be Legendary Leadership Conference near Chicago. This conference uniquely featured eight amazing keynote speakers. As much as I am passionate about delivering my own rousing and informative keynotes, I am also delighted any time I get to watch other experienced speakers go through their programs. As a speaking coach, I am a raving fan of well-delivered speeches. I was thrilled when the event organizers told me that my keynote was later in the afternoon, giving me a front-row seat (literally) to seven other outstanding speeches. As each talented speaker moved through her or his respective leadership keynotes, I was treated to a master class in storytelling.

For eight hours, I sat enthralled by the stories that were being shared. The day started with leadership consultant Barbara Wichman rebounding from a crushing defeat in her 6th-grade class presidency to becoming an accomplished leader in a major retail firm. TV and radio host Jeanne Sparrow shared heartfelt stories about her father helping her to lean into fear. Adventurer and record-holder Suzanne Nance had me mesmerized as she recalled near-death experiences while summiting Mt. Everest. The day wrapped with the fabulous Sarah Victory leading us through her harrowing experience of being carjacked by a scared 15-year-old boy. Over and over, I gasped, cried, laughed, and rejoiced while I also gained leadership and life lessons. That magical day showcased the undeniable importance of story. Learning to use stories effectively is such a pivotal piece of sales, leadership, and speaking, leading us to **Invincible Principle 5: Share Great Stories**.

Most every one of us were raised listening and growing through stories. For me, I remember reading stories with my mom at a very young age. Eventually, I started telling them to others. I got lots of storytelling practice. I would tell stories to my friends and other kids at school. As a teenager, we would take turns telling stories whenever our parents let us build a campfire. At some point, I learned to start playing with my delivery for maximum effect. I would slow down and lower my voice to draw my friends in, then suddenly yell, laughing victoriously as they screamed in terror. If this all sounds familiar to your own experience, more than likely, you also have a love for the hearing and telling of great stories.

Despite our affinity for stories, for some inexplicable reason, when given the task of selling, leading, or speaking to others in the workplace, we all but abandon our innate storytelling skills. This results in most sales and workplace presentations falling into the trap of just being hours-long recitations of facts and information. Perhaps this is because we assume any work presentation must stay "professional," mistakenly thinking a work setting is no place for something we enjoyed as a kid. In working with my clients, I have also found that many experienced salespeople and leaders struggle to feel confident when telling stories in this context. This includes a recent client, a CEO of a non-profit, who shared, "I am so much more comfortable talking about the services we provide than I am telling stories." This resulted in my creating a simple Success Plan consisting of four words: **Fewer services, more stories.**

If you are reading this book, you are a storyteller. If your brain resists that notion, it is time to get used to it. Storytelling is simply the sharing of ideas and experiences in such a way that those ideas will resonate with others. Storytelling is a part of who you are; it is in your DNA. You can either continue to resist that fact, or you can embrace it and use it to your fullest advantage. As change is affecting every organization on the planet, it becomes even more essential that salespeople and leaders use storytelling to cut through the complexity and make these changes understandable.

Most of us have been sharing stories with family and friends throughout our entire lives, making **storytelling synonymous with building relationships.** Dan Giancola, Chief Financial Officer at DoubleGood, spoke to this truth: "Automation doesn't feel authentic. Technology has made things so busy. Which is why it comes back around to human interaction." A cornerstone of human interaction is sharing ideas and experiences through storytelling.

It is no surprise that the most popular content on social media is recorded and live videos. A 2016 study conducted by internet networking giant Cisco estimated that video streaming and downloads would make up over 80% of all internet traffic by 2022. This number will undoubtedly continue to grow. While online video has multiple factors contributing to its appeal, one of the leading ones is that video can convey a story in ways that GIFs, text, and images cannot.

In the last chapter, we walked through your strong opening, clear solution, and compelling close. As you strive to speak with impact, the final powerful component needed is the use of great stories, so let us better understand how to discover, develop, and deliver stories effectively.

Discovering Stories Around You

One of the most common statements I hear from clients is, "I don't have any stories. Where do they come from?" To which I simply reply, "Everywhere." Each day, interesting events and insightful experiences are happening to you. Unless the experience was so noteworthy you could never forget it, most of these daily experiences will fade from your memory. However, by training yourself to be always on the hunt for good stories, you will find that many of those daily experiences could be used to highlight a lesson that you learned or knowledge you gained.

Going further, interesting experiences are not limited to what happens with customers, coworkers, or other work situations. Events and experiences from home, with family and friends, or in your community groups could also be used to demonstrate a key point during your meetings and presentations. Even experiences that may seem random or meaningless at first may contain hidden lessons you can use to your advantage.

Where do you start to look for good stories to include in your presentations and talks? Certainly, there are obvious choices. **Among the most effective stories for salespeople and leaders are success stories.** In sales, new customers will be looking for proof that they will not be your first customer of their size and in their industry. New customers also want to know in what ways you have helped others. A well-placed customer success story will build confidence that you can deliver your offering in the way that you are claiming and give a better understanding of the services that you provide. Instead of just rattling off a list of companies with whom you have worked, use a customer success story to best illustrate your experience and capabilities.

Success stories are useful for leaders as well. Think back to the example of Tammy, the CEO of a mid-sized organization. Once she understood what stories to look for, Tammy quickly discovered 2-3 stories she could sprinkle into her keynote. One story described how a team of hers had gone above and beyond to serve one of their customers in an unexpected way. This story was perfect because she was able to use it to demonstrate successful customer service and successful team collaboration.

Another useful story is your "Why" story and the "Why" of your company. Why did you choose this company or this industry for your career? Why are you so passionate about your products and services? Why was your company founded? Why does your company have the mission that it does? Use of a "Why" story to share your background will create an even greater sense of connection because storytelling makes you and your company relatable.

It is worth noting that in the last chapter I cautioned against using the first few minutes of your talk to discuss your credentials and your company's many awards. To clarify, your customer or audience does want to know some background details about you and your company. You can use a "Why" story as one method to share your background. I suggest moving that story later in your presentation, enabling your strong opening to remain all about them.

An example of where a "Why" story would be useful came out during a conversation with Howard Diamond, Chief Strategy Officer at Rise Interactive. As we talked, I asked Howard why he pushes himself as a leader. Howard responded, "If you are good at sales and you work for the right company, you will create jobs for people. There's a sense of pride in building a company from eight people to over two hundred and fifty. We're not just selling to sell. We're creating jobs. People are buying houses and having kids. This gives me a tremendous sense of pride to add to people's lives." Howard's response has everything needed to make a great "Why" story that would help us better know his organization and feel a stronger connection to him.

As you look to discover stories that may be useful, look for stories that will evoke emotion in your intended audience. No, I do not suggest you try to make your clients cry. But you do want them to *feel*. As author Paul Smith points out in *Sell with a Story*, "Storytelling speaks to the part of the brain where decisions are actually made." Smith explains that cognitive science shows that people often make "subconscious, emotional... decisions in one place in the brain, then justify those decisions rationally or logically in another place." This means that the right story will move your audience farther along the journey into a new way of thinking. Being aware of the emotional power of storytelling, you are better able to lead your audience to a place where they want to take action.

As you explore what stories you can utilize in your sales, leadership, and speaking career, a few points of clarity. **Stories should be genuine.** Something you can proudly stand behind. Is it okay to change the date of a customer success story from 2016 to 2019? That seems harmless enough. However, I would caution against changing the fundamental elements of what really happened unless it is to protect a customer's identity or another equally important reason. You never want to be in a situation where you get caught in a lie and lose your customer's or team's trust. Also, stories should not be manipulative. Share stories that will help you demonstrate a key point or highlight your work, not to coax the customer into making a purchase they are not ready to make. **Remember, above all else, you are there to serve. Let your authenticity shine through as you share stories with others.**

Success Step

Take several moments to write down 3-5 story ideas that you would like to develop. You only need an idea for now. In the next section, we will explore whether your ideas can turn into great stories. (Spoiler Alert: Not all of them will!) For now, let yourself discover whatever story ideas you have. What is a customer success that you can turn into a story that will showcase your organization and your unique offering? Think of a time when a customer was really struggling with an issue in his business and your solution made a significant difference. What is one story that you could share that speaks to you or your company's passion for helping others? Was there a time when you faced a setback but learned an important lesson? Rather than just listing your credentials, what story would better help us get to know you?

Over time, I encourage you to discover even more stories that will be useful for you in a range of sales or leadership situations. Shoot for 8-10 stories that you are comfortable with telling. As stories are everywhere, always be ready for a story idea to occur. When a story pops into your head, immediately stop what you are doing and make some notes. Use a paper notebook or keep notes on your phone using OneNote, Evernote, or any notes app. Better still, use a voice memo app to record yourself talking through your story idea. Do not let the moment pass without jotting something down because that great idea may not be in your head later. **Life is full of stories. We want to hear yours!**

Developing Your Stories

Now that you are starting to collect your story ideas, it is time to develop them into something useable and effective. But first, it is time to answer the question, "How do I know if my idea will make a good story?"

Great stories consist of these elements:

1. Time
2. Place
3. Main Character
4. Challenge
5. Defining Moment
6. Lesson

1. Time – **To add context, give your audience perspective on when the events of your story occurred.** Be as specific as necessary to convey an approximate time without unnecessary detail. For example, "In March of 2020, I met with a customer…" or "Last year, my team was facing…" Other indicators such as "One night recently, I had an idea…" or "Every fall, one of our customers…" Avoid details such as "It was

March sixth of 2019 around three-thirty in the afternoon…" unless that specific date and time is important to what is about to unfold.

2. Place – Like the time element, **including an indicator of "where" helps those listening to picture the setting in their minds.** The audience does not have to have been to that specific location before. When you set the location "In a large conference room" or "Touring my client's data center," most of us will immediately get pictures in our mind. Once again, less is more here. "The room had blue walls and stiff-backed chairs" are details we do not need unless the point of your story involves color schemes and furniture selections.

3. Main Character – **Every good story needs one key player we can follow through the events of the story.** In sales and leadership stories, most of the time this is one person, although sometimes there are more. The main character could be a customer contact, a peer, a partner, or yourself. Though some stories involve companies themselves, focusing on an individual helps us to personalize the story. "I met with Mary, the VP of Sales at Acme Widgets," for example. Though we have never met the actual Mary at Acme Widgets, our minds will draw upon people in our own lives to picture her. This helps us better connect with your story and root for her success.

4. Challenge – **What is standing in the way of your main character achieving his or her goal?** Is it a bad leader? A struggling market? Is there a competitor that is luring away their customers? Sometimes the challenge is internal, such as lack of confidence, disorganization, or an impending deadline. Great stories will use emotion to help us feel this challenge ourselves. "If I didn't get my team pulled together, we'd miss our deadline, resulting in a two-million-dollar loss. This would be disastrous for our growing company." Because of its role in adding an emotional connection with your audience, be sure the challenge in the story is clearly defined and relatable.

5. Defining Moment – **Your story builds to this pivotal event.** This is the moment in your story where the main character comes face to face with the challenge itself. After this defining moment, your main character is changed forever. There can be no lesson learned without this confrontation. This means that the climax of the story is the most important element. Will Mary get the deal or will her competition win? When faced with a career-defining decision, does the employee learn how to be a team player? After years of stagnation, did the company give up or recommit to the values that made it successful years earlier? By building to this most important moment, you have the audience on the edge of their seats.

6. Lesson – **What is the audience supposed to learn from your story?** What is the takeaway that you want the customer to have? The lesson of the story should align with the outcome you are trying to drive home. Sometimes this will be abundantly clear, while other times the lesson is less obvious. Because of this, to avoid misinterpretation, make sure you articulate the lesson clearly.

Now that you understand the key elements of good sales and leadership stories, use these elements to build out your story. I prefer to do this on paper (or the electronic equivalent). Doing your initial story development only in your head may lead to confusion and make you prone to forget elements you wanted to add.

I start by writing out what lesson I want the audience to take away from the story. By starting with the lesson, I better understand how to develop the story by keeping the main takeaway in mind. I want my audience to easily connect the dots between the story and the lesson. For example, I tell a brief story about unwittingly poisoning the roots of a tree in my yard in my attempt to prevent grass and weeds from growing around the base of the tree. After telling the story, I finish with, "Now, whenever I look at that tree, I ask myself, 'What am I doing to protect my own roots?'" Developing the story with the **lesson** in mind will ensure it stays on track.

Next, create an outline of the story, making sure to include the six key elements. Once the outline is in place, take another pass to write out more complete ideas on what to say. Decide if you want to write out the entire story or leave it as an outline. Some people do not write down every word because they feel this makes them appear as if they were reciting lines. However, at first, I tend to write out new stories completely while I remain open to changes and improvisation as I practice. You decide what process works best for you.

When it comes to adding details, stick to the relevant ones while discarding the unimportant or distracting ones. Remember, unnecessary details not only make your story needlessly long, but they also result in listeners struggling to remember the important facts. To be effective, keep things minimal by only including what is needed to drive the story forward. For every sentence of the story, ask "What point does this sentence serve?" If you cannot clearly define a point for each sentence, then it can probably be dropped.

A good length to strive for is 1-2 minutes per story because most key details and the main point or lesson can typically be conveyed in 1-2 minutes. This is not a rule. I have seen incredible speakers tell great stories in as little as 30 seconds or as long as 3-4 minutes or more. If you are new to storytelling in your meetings and presentations, start out with shorter stories and expand as you feel more comfortable. Keeps your stories tight for maximum effect. Ultimately, if each detail in the story adds value and you can hold your audience's attention, the story is a winner!

Success Step

Keeping the six key elements in mind, create an outline for each of your story ideas. Remember to include references to time and place for helpful context. Identify the main character to whom the audience can relate. Define the challenge (the bigger the better) and add tension as the main character works her way toward the defining moment. Once the main character faces that defining moment, make sure the audience knows what the key lesson is in your story. With the structure defined, continue to work on the story to develop its greatness.

The Magic is in Your Delivery

In the opening moment of her powerful and brilliant 2014 TED Talk, Mellody Hobson, the president of Ariel Investments, shares a compelling story. I highly recommend it for anyone looking to watch a great speech. To open her talk, Mellody describes a business trip to New York City in 2006 in which a stranger assumed she was the hired help based on the color of her skin.

That story is a perfect example of what great stories can do. In just over one minute, Mellody's story grabs my attention, gets me emotionally invested, shocks me in that one defining moment, and instills in me an important lesson. She appears comfortable on stage. Just like Mellody, you will soon be delivering great stories to customers, employees, or any audience you choose.

To deliver powerful stories, you need three things: The story itself, practice, and an audience. In a moment we will go through several practice techniques. Before we do, one more key piece of advice could mean the difference between a good story and a great one. As you start to practice your stories, you must remain open to adjusting them to be as effective as possible. This may include removing details that you *love* about one of the stories. You may have heard the term "kill your darlings," which speaks to a storyteller's or writer's need to discard some beloved aspects of the story. You must be willing to make tough choices to make certain you do not slow down the energy of a presentation or disrupt the flow of the main idea.

Many times, I have developed a new story, refining it down to what I thought were the essential details, only to realize the story took too long to tell. When this happens, my brain clings to every precious detail in my story. I think, "No! Every word here is essential. I can't cut anything or else they won't 'get it.'" Yet, time and time again, when I force myself to cut out "precious" details, I soon see that they were not needed at all. The main idea becomes even clearer and the presentation flow is enhanced, which helps my audience to stay engaged. This illustrates that the more you practice and share stories, they will become as great as they can be only if you are willing to kill a few darlings along the way.

This brings us to practice. When it comes to growing your skills, there is no substitute for practice. Just as going to a gym on a regular basis is required to develop muscles and continuous learning is required to grow your knowledge, the same is true for improving your speaking skills. This is especially true in storytelling as it is often something you are not used to doing in workplace meetings and sales pitches. Practice will remain an important element in a great delivery.

Some choose to perfect the delivery of stories "on the fly," by just trying them out in front of customers. Although this is not a terrible approach, most of the time when we are presenting in front of others, our heads are filled with many things. "Are my slides working?" "Are they paying attention?" "Are they going to buy anything?" "Why did that person check her phone; is she bored?" "Is there any salad from lunch stuck in my teeth?" With all this going on in our heads, it is hard to get a gauge on whether one story may be effective or not. I will always advocate for deliberate practice on your own or in front of a few trusted peers or friends.

This does not take a great deal of time or effort. As each of your stories is only a few minutes long, they are easy to practice while doing laps around the track at the gym, while being stuck in traffic, or while in the shower. Whenever possible, speak the stories out loud. (You will learn to ignore your fellow commuters' strange looks, I promise.) By speaking out loud, you are more likely to catch grammatical errors or phrases that are hard to say. In addition, speaking the stories out loud will help to simplify the details and sound more natural over time. I will admit, when doing laps around the track, I am not speaking my stories out loud, but you are very likely to see my lips moving! I also make sure to practice in my office or while driving, which enables me the privacy of being able to talk them out.

As you get more comfortable with them, grab your mobile phone and record yourself going through the story. I know, I know, just the suggestion of recording yourself on video has already caused a bead of sweat to form on your upper lip. But come on now, you can do it! Prop your phone against something (coffee mugs were great for phone-tilting) and stand about 6 feet away. Go through the story two or three times, then play it back, listening for areas where something sounds unclear or where you may have had a difficult time. What can be made even better? Another option is for you to practice in front of the bathroom or hallway mirror. I always suggest using a recording wherever possible, but the mirror will do if you do not have a phone handy.

With enough practice under your belt, you are now ready to get those stories in front of an audience. To ensure your success, use these suggestions to deliver your stories powerfully:

1. The Lead-in – **Do not start with, "Let me tell you a story…"** As much as the audience loves stories, we often bristle at the thought of being told we are going to hear a story. Your audience may associate the word "story" with "fake" or "child-like." Instead, use a lead-in such as, "One recent example of this is…" or "I was in a similar situation two years ago…" Oftentimes, you do not need a lead-in. Just start telling the story.

2. Eye Contact – **Eye contact connects us to our audience.** While this applies to the entire presentation, having good eye contact is always important while telling a story. Many speakers tend to move their eyes across the audience, scanning the room. Instead, draw the audience in by locking eyes with individual attendees for 3-5 seconds each before moving to someone else. This is a must to keep connection with your audience.

3. Involve Your Audience – **Use connection to draw the audience in.** As mentioned in the last chapter, use questions strategically, even during a story. Tell a key detail and then ask, "Has anyone had that happen to them?" Do not forget to use the first names of people in attendance during the story. For example, "Two months ago, my banking customer came to me. Just like [insert attendee name] mentioned earlier, this customer had the same issue you folks do in wanting your remote employees..." Even when telling stories about others, keep the focus on those in the room.

Beyond these suggestions, how you use stories is up to you. As you share them with others, keep asking for feedback. Explore what is working well and adjust as needed. Do not be afraid to make hard choices to remove details when needed. Over time, with practice and delivery, stories become a powerful and effective way to make your presentations and meetings soar!

Invincible Tips

1. You are a storyteller. We all are
2. Storytelling is synonymous with building relationships
3. Start with 3-5 stories, then expand to 8-10 stories you are ready to deliver
4. Use success stories to reassure customers that you can address their needs
5. Great storytelling takes practice and feedback

Summary

Think of the speakers that you admire the most. Perhaps you are inspired by speakers like Brené Brown, Gary Vaynerchuk, Les Brown, or others. Maybe your role model is someone closer to you, such as the CEO of your company or a regional manager who tells stories with ease. **No matter who inspires you, know that right now, at this very moment, there are people out in the world searching for someone to inspire them. Make it you!**

Always be looking to discover new stories, keeping a notebook of possible story ideas. Develop stories by mapping out the key elements in an outline before refining them into a full story. Finally, use practice and effective speaking techniques to bring your story to life. Regardless of your position, speaking experience, or current confidence level, soon you will be delivering amazing stories to customers and peers.

Great stories, along with great storytelling, make great speakers.

INVINCIBLE PRINCIPLE 6: FOSTER LASTING BELIEF

"It's the repetition of affirmations that leads to belief. And once that belief becomes a deep conviction, things begin to happen."
— Muhammad Ali

In looking back at the first five principles, we see that Principles 1-3 are foundational components. They are qualities and practices that we should be utilizing to develop solid relationships with those we serve. Building on that foundation, Principles 4 and 5 present the best opportunity to create a unique and memorable experience when serving our customers and employees. These two principles are about moving people to take action. **Once you put these principles into practice, you will immediately start to increase connection, engagement, and action.**

Yet there is one final principle that is essential to reaching Invincible Success. Without it, any education, experience, and training will fall short of what is needed to be prosperous. You will find yourself frequently stuck in place, unsure how best to proceed. This one principle alone acts as an accelerant to goals and ambitions. It wraps itself around the other five principles and your relentless determination, magnifying their effectiveness. It will provide clarity in the face of uncertainty and resolve in the face of difficulty. Rounding out the steps to your success is **Invincible Principle 6: Develop Lasting Belief**.

Lasting belief may seem like a surprising principle to include in a book that has a chapter on the perils of Impostor Syndrome. I will admit, years ago, I would not have been able to write a complete chapter on belief. At times, it felt like I may not be able to write a complete sentence on belief. However, through awareness and simple changes to my daily practices, I have been able to put those days of uncertainty behind me and cultivate an enthusiastic, positive perspective on my abilities. Situations that used to cause me to tear myself down or question my chances of success now invigorate and excite me at the potential they afford. The same can be true for you. **No matter what experiences you have had with self-belief in the past, you can tap into the limitless potential of belief.**

Even beyond my own experiences with belief, many of the leaders I interviewed made specific references to belief in their own careers. One example was Rich Wood, Vice President of Alliances at Rightpoint, who shared, "By believing in my abilities, I know I am more effective." Rich reminds us to "**believe that your experience is a valuable market commodity.**" Leader after leader echoed these sentiments.

Belief does not just determine our success; it transforms the quality of our life. Early in this book, I spoke about a rock-climbing scene from *Mission: Impossible 2*. I described Ethan Hunt dangling off the edge of a cliff. There is an equally exhilarating and terrifying rock-climbing example that showcases the potential of belief. It is also *entirely real*. On the morning of June 3, 2017, climber Alex Honnold stood at the base of a massive rock formation known as "El Capitan." "El Cap," as it's affectionately called, is the Holy Grail of rock climbing. Located in Yosemite National Park, El Cap is a 3,200-foot-tall slab of sheer granite that is widely considered to be the most difficult and dangerous rock in the world. That morning, Alex did not slip on a safety harness or tie himself into a rope of any kind. Using no equipment at all except for shoes and a bag of powdered chalk to keep his fingers dry, Alex began to climb.

Until that day, even the most elite and skilled climbers in the world considered it impossible to free solo (climb with no safety equipment) El Cap. In fact, most climbers would consider an attempt to free solo El Cap to be an act of insanity. Yet Alex Honnold believed. He believed in his training, believed in his body, and believed in his mindset. Because of that belief, after just 3 hours and 56 minutes of climbing, Alex safely reached the top of El Cap. Later, he was asked about what role belief has in his life. Alex responded, "I feel that a lot of human spirituality stems from the belief that we are unique and special in the universe." Which raises the question, what is your relationship with belief?

Some people let their belief in themselves, or lack thereof, drive their decisions. However, you can take control of belief. **By fostering a lasting belief in our skills, tenacity, and endless capacity to achieve, we can accomplish greatness.**

When I became more intentional in three specific areas, I was able to refocus my self-belief. To unlock the tremendous potential of belief in my life, I took control of **my growth, my gratitude, and the story I tell myself.**

Achieving Big Growth

For most of our life, well-intentioned people, from our parents to our teachers, managers, friends, and mentors, have all been telling us that we need to have goals, right? Our social media feeds are plastered with colorful and profound sayings about goals and goal-setting. Every self-help book we read or podcast we listen to reminds us to take on BHAGs (Big Hairy Audacious Goals). I added my voice to this cacophony of reminders all the way back in Chapter 1 when I had you write down what goals you will achieve when you are Invincible!

It seems clear that having clear goals for our day and our life is important. After all, without goals, we are apt to wander in life, just letting life happen. Without daily goals, we are prone to distractions in our day, chasing the "shiny objects" or "squirrels" that scamper across our path. Have you ever found yourself heading to YouTube to watch one helpful video to get you started on a task, only to spin into a multi-hour spiral of cat videos? Setting and striving for goals helps limit these frustrating scenarios.

Beyond just *setting* goals, you can make certain to *achieve* those goals. To do that, I suggest you concentrate not just on where you want to go but also the system you put in place to get you there. Each step you take toward the target means that you are growing. **Growth unleashes a thirst for more growth.** You will get energized about the progress you are making, resulting in pushing for more. By emphasizing the transformation process itself, we learn to celebrate both the journey and the destination. This makes any big goal attainable.

This powerful process was the subject of my 2019 TEDx Talk. (Watch the full talk at invinciblesuccess.com/media.) Here is an excerpt:

> When it comes to your big goals, ask yourself, are you accomplishing them? Research shows that many of us do not. How many of you have ever made a New Year's resolution? Many of us have, me included. Yet, a 2013 University of Scranton study found that of those that do make resolutions, only 8% actually stick with them long enough to achieve the goal. Why is that? Why don't we accomplish every big goal? Some might say, "It's because I make my goals too big." That's not it. Most of the time, our goals are too small. We routinely limit what we're capable of because we don't yet believe we can do something so big. **The problem of us not accomplishing every big goal we want to accomplish isn't that our goals are too big. It's that we make the steps to accomplish those goals too big.**
>
> Of course, I'm not the first person to say that. We've all heard the sayings, "The journey of a thousand miles begins

with a single step" or "How do you eat an elephant? One bite at a time!" But I don't know what that means. I have no plans to walk a thousand miles or eat an elephant. So, like many others, in the past, I'd make big goals with the best of intentions, yet rarely follow through. Then I discovered the power of small steps. Unfortunately, it was because there came a time in my life when small steps were all I could take.

Several years ago, I was not in great shape. I was more than 20 pounds overweight. My diet was embarrassing, and I avoided exercise. I always told myself, "I'm just fine," so I didn't see any reason to change. That was until after a routine surgery. The surgery itself went fine, but because I didn't take better care of myself, I didn't heal. One week after surgery, I suffered a major complication and I started bleeding. A lot. I was rushed to the hospital, where they immediately started transfusing blood back into my body. But I was losing fluid faster than they could put it in. Between the transfusions and my own blood, the doctors estimate that I lost the equivalent of 80% of my blood. With no warning whatsoever, I had gone from "just fine" to "just about dead." Finally, I was hurried into the operating room. Five hours later, when I woke up, I knew I was lucky to be alive. I also knew I wanted to make big changes in my health.

But where should I begin? I didn't know. After what happened, I could hardly move. So, one morning, a few weeks after I came home from the hospital, I drank a glass of water. That's it. Nothing more. I had read somewhere that drinking a glass of water first thing in the morning jumpstarts your metabolism and makes you feel full. I thought, "I probably can't screw up a glass of water." So, I did that. Every morning when I woke up, I drank a full glass of water. That is the only change I made.

After about a month of this, I was standing in the kitchen basking in the glow of having successfully drunk my daily *glass of water when I thought, "You know, you're feeling a little better. You're just standing here. Maybe you could do a little exercise." I did a few crunches and then added those to my morning routine. Over the next several months, with no planning beforehand, as I felt stronger and stronger, I added sit ups, then I added pushups, and eventually added planks. To go along with the exercise, I started making small but continuous changes to my diet. I changed my breakfast of Pop-tarts and energy drinks to healthy smoothies and lots of water. I was losing weight and felt amazing.*

That excerpt describes the beginning of the significant change I underwent in terms of finding ways to grow every day. As I described earlier in the book, years ago, I struggled with Impostor Syndrome, which led to depression and nearly ended my marriage. Because of the success I had in taking small steps to improve my health each day, I started expanding my "grow every day" mindset to my relationships, physical health, and more. This helped me to discover and implement new daily routines. It also helped me come to know that we can radically reshape our life simply by taking small growth steps each day.

How? First, decide on the big goal you would like to accomplish. Once you have that locked in, figure out *something* you can do that should move you towards your goal. **Decide on a small step you can take.** Do not waste time trying to figure out the perfect first step. **Remember, the perfect first step is the one you take.**

Once you have a step small enough for you to get started, then it is a matter of building that step into your life. To do that, James Clear, author of the book *Atomic Habits*, recommends the three R's of making habits stick: Reminder, Routine, and Reward.

- **Reminder** - Do not try to count on memory to try to take new steps. Set reminders on your phone or hang up sticky notes.

- **Routine** – The more routine you make the small step, the more likely it will stick. Do it the same time every day. If you miss a day or two or three, get right back at it.
- **Reward** – When we accomplish something, even small steps, we feel a sense of satisfaction. Take time to celebrate that. Do not wait to complete the big goal. It is the *growth* you are after, so acknowledge those little wins.

Once the step becomes dependable, it is time to take another small step. **Step by step, over time, you can achieve any big goal.**

 Success Step

Decide what small step you will take next to achieve growth. Align it with your Invincible goals. This growth step should move you toward your larger goal, even if only a little. Once you determine that small step, commit to taking this growth step every day for one month. If you struggle, do your best to try it for one week. If you determine the step is too big to do each day, pick a smaller step. Over time, when that small step becomes a habit, it is time for a new step. When you grow every day, you make any goal possible.

Most leaders develop daily habits that provide discipline around personal growth. Bryan Ritter from Sprinklr sees his personal growth as a tremendous opportunity, saying "I must be willing to bend and reshape in order to grow." Riccardo Leite from Dell looks for chances to grow with "Living by example, learning all the time, including failure." Still others see growth in the intangible, including Thad Fisher of Netrix, who told me, "Paying it forward is a very big thing for me. Part of my growth is making sure I do what I can to make someone smile each day."

What step will you take as you strive for growth?

CELEBRATE WITH GRATITUDE

Growing up, my mother taught me the value of good manners. Because of her, for my entire life, I have rarely asked for something without using "Please." In fact, I often find myself having to spend extra time editing my work emails because I overuse the word "please," including more than one in the same sentence. Still, if one might think I'm a bit heavy-handed on the "please," that is nothing compared to the number of times I say "thank you." While saying "thank you" was instilled in me from a very young age, it was not until I received a seemingly ordinary gift from my daughter Cassidy a few years ago that I came to understand what living with gratitude really can do for your life.

I am a hard person to shop for. For many years, I have driven my family crazy on most gift-giving occasions because "I really can't think of anything I need." I am proud of myself when I come up with exciting suggestions like t-shirts or socks or more dry-erase markers. Which is why I was surprised when, shortly before I started my own speaking and consulting business, Cassidy gave me the gift of a journal for Father's Day, encouraging me to write down ideas for my new business. I playfully asked, "What if I never have any?" Ignoring my Dad humor, Cassidy said, "Then write down what you're grateful for."

The gratitude idea stuck with me. A few months later, I sat down to reflect on my day. That first night, and every night since, I have written three things I was grateful for on that given day. In the last few moments before turning the lights off to go to sleep, I sit on the side of my bed and capture three things for which I am thankful. I will admit, there are some nights when I need an extra minute to try to think of three things. With just a little extra reflection, I have always managed to find at least three. Most days, there are plenty of moments in my day from which to choose. On the truly amazing days, I bend the rules and write down a fourth item, but I generally stick to the top three. Line by line, page after page, and now journal after journal, my world has become filled with gratitude.

In the nearly three years since I started the nightly practice, I have close to 3,000 experiences, events, and moments of appreciation captured in my journals. That is journals with an 's' because after filling my first journal, I am into the second (another gift!). Pages filled with moments of gratitude for my wife, my two kids, my mom, father, brothers, my wife's family, friends, peers, and other important people in my life. Even Riley, our goofy dog, has made it in the journal on numerous occasions. I write down grateful moments in my career and the amazing people I have had the good fortune to meet. Big moments like being grateful to stand on stage, serving hundreds of amazing audience members. I also include the little things I am grateful for, such as a day without my arm aching after months of recovery from an injury or being outside to watch the sun come up during my morning jog.

Beyond the quiet chance to reflect at night, I soon got a surprise. **I discovered this nightly exercise was training my brain to be looking for moments of happiness at all times.** Experiences that would normally fly by without hardly a thought were now being acknowledged and celebrated. Since I did not have my journal with me, I found myself pausing to savor those moments more than ever before, allowing myself to take them in fully in order to remember them better that night. My brain became a gratitude detector, always on the hunt for more positive beliefs.

Even more unexpectedly was what a profound effect this came to have on my self-belief. **Not only was I taking in more that was happening in the world outside of myself, but I became much more in tune with my own personal strengths and accomplishments.** I became even more grateful for the chance to help others, both in small and large ways. Grateful for my abilities as a speaker, to connect and move an audience. Grateful for my health, my ability to stay calm in moments of chaos, and my tenacity in the face of resistance.

Over time, I have found that not only had I trained myself to always be on the hunt for moments of gratitude, but I was soon receiving even more reason to celebrate than what I would have experienced otherwise. In other words, I was not just *seeing* more instances of the good things in my life, *more of them were happening*. Case in point, when I started giving handwritten notes to individuals thanking them for a recent meeting, to my surprise, I found that those individuals were responding by introducing me to other important people in their network. This led to more amazing conversations, more confidence, and so on.

The leaders I have worked with and interviewed are quick to share their own focus on gratitude. In Episode 15 of the *Invincible Success* podcast, I interviewed Marcus Anderson, an author, speaker, and mindset coach. Marcus told me "Gratitude is not passive. Gratitude is powerful. It's an action. We should be out there doing things that show gratitude." Radio host Geetha Krishnan not only embodies Marcus' words, but she also takes them to another level. She once shared with me that she writes dozens of moments a day for which she is grateful, sometimes over a hundred a day. What a wonderful over-achiever!

By being thankful, my business took off and became more fulfilling. Living with gratitude became my single greatest source of building self-belief in all I am meant to do.

Success Step

Take a few moments each day to reflect on those things for which you are grateful. Find at least three things for which you are grateful and write them down. Create your own journal of gratitude moments from your life. By capturing them, you are creating a living testament of examples in your life where good things happened to you, large and small. **Filling your life with gratitude will be a powerful force for building belief in your skills, choices, and what life has to offer.**

Believing Is Seeing

The final and most essential component of belief is the story you tell yourself. Regardless of whether the chapter on Impostor Syndrome resonated with you, for most of us, there are times in life when we have been less than kind to ourselves. Too often, we place idealistic expectations on ourselves, only to grow frustrated when we do not exceed these improbable standards. This may stem from incidents from our past, or we may subconsciously measure ourselves against peers or friends. Regardless of circumstances and past experiences, there is no reason to continue being a passive listener to your inner dialog. Instead, take an active role in shaping that ongoing story happening within.

Nearly everyone has heard the expression, "Seeing is believing." This is a favorite of anyone who, before they will believe it is possible, must see tangible proof. If I said that one year from now your small business will be making over $1 million dollars a year in revenue, would you roll your eyes and reply, "I'll believe that when I see it"? What if you have had the expression wrong all this time? What if the truth is that you start to achieve your desired results only after you believe they are possible? In other words, stop allowing your life to be a matter of "Seeing is believing." **Instead, live a life of "Believing is seeing."**

To me, "Believing is seeing" is the idea of believing your success into existence. It is the practice of being intentional about what you tell yourself every day for the purpose of shaping what happens in your life and career. Make no mistake, what you tell yourself *will* come true. It does not matter if what you are telling yourself is good, bad, or ugly. It will still come true. As well-known salesman and leader Henry Ford once said, **"Whether you think you can, or you think you can't – you're right."** That is because the mind is such an incredible resource. It is constantly at work on our behalf. **Every second we are awake (and even some when we sleep), our brain is strategizing on our behalf to manifest more of what we seek.** Knowing this gives you a chance to remove the clutter of thoughts that derail your progress and gives you an incredible opportunity to make great things come to life.

As a former Microsoft employee, I have always had a great deal of respect for what Bill Gates has accomplished. Not only did he create an undeniably successful enterprise, but he went on to become one of the world's greatest philanthropists. In my first year at Microsoft, I had the unique opportunity to accompany Mr. Gates to an elementary school on Chicago's south side and take pictures of him meeting with some of the students. While watching him interact with those young kids, it seemed as if his brain was working differently than most. A few months ago, I watched a Netflix documentary called *Inside Bill's Brain*. In the first episode, Bill tells us, "You have to pick a pretty finite number of things to tell your mind to work on."

Ask yourself, "What am I going to tell my brain to work on today?" Do not leave it to chance. Instead, train your brain to work on only those things that bring you growth and accomplishment. A very powerful way to do this is by using aspirational phrases. The great news is it only takes about three minutes a day!

Several years ago, during the peak of my struggle with Impostor Syndrome, I was searching for more ways to improve my self-belief. I found an internet article from author and speaker Jack Canfield discussing the Law of Attraction. Simply put, the Law of Attraction says that you will attract into your life whatever you focus on. That is when I first realized that believing is seeing!

Reading that article, I decide to make a list of my strengths and start reading it out loud each morning. At first, I wrote such things as, "I am a good listener. I am organized. I am ambitious." However, over time, I found myself adding to the list. I added, "I am a strong team player. I am a good father." One day I wrote, "I am… Invincible." By changing my focus, I was changing my beliefs, which in turn has changed my life. **Now, years after my lowest moment, by believing in myself, I have recommitted to my wife, reconnected with my children, and completely reconstructed my career.**

I created a practice each morning to spend just a few minutes focusing my brain on delivering those successes I most seek. I now read aspirations such as, "I am serving over 1 million people a year through my speaking programs" and "I am serving myself when I serve others" and "I am leaning into challenge, pushing forward, even when afraid." This morning ritual has not only activated my brain in ways I had not previously thought possible, but it has dramatically improved the positivity of my inner dialog. Because belief is the foundation on which I start my days, I see the proof as I grow and exceed my goals.

 **Success Step**

Write your own list of aspirational statements. Write 5-8 statements that you aspire to achieve in your life. Use phrases such as "I am…" "I will…" "I have…" or "I serve others by…" As before, do not limit your statements to only those aspirations you *know* you can make happen. As you write, move beyond goals, writing statements about the values you aspire to convey. What kind of person do you strive to be? How will you impact others?

With your list written, spend 3 minutes at the beginning of your day reading the list of aspirational statements. Over time, as your belief and confidence build, stretch this to 10-15 aspirational statements. Allow your aspirations to grow and change as you reach new levels of success.

Reading your aspirational statements at the start of your day will make certain you feel uplifted and energized to go after your goals. Still, there can be moments during your day when your confidence or purpose is wavering. Perhaps you are about to go into an important customer meeting, employee review, or step out on stage. There are any number of situations when we may want to inject a quick moment of affirmation into our day—something I call a "Belief Boost." To do this, develop a brief mantra for yourself that you can quickly recite to get an injection of confidence. Just a sentence or two that you can use to center yourself and remind yourself, "I got this!"

For me, when I am moments from stepping out on stage to serve others, I give myself a Belief Boost using my Invincible mantra. I find a quiet spot where I can close my eyes. I take two slow, deep breaths and quietly say, "**I am confident, I have purpose, and I speak with impact. Therefore, I am Invincible!**" Repeating this mantra to myself once or twice gives me the focus and energy to go out and deliver. You are welcome to use this mantra for yourself or develop one that is more meaningful and effective for you. Use it the next time you are in need of a boost.

Train your brain to focus on those things to which you aspire to unleash limitless growth and a positive mindset. Use aspirational statements to start each day by instructing your brain to discover answers to your sales and leadership challenges. Soon you will discover new ways to serve your customers, empower your team, and delight your audiences. When you believe, you will see.

INVINCIBLE TIPS

1. Tap into the limitless potential of belief
2. Achieve big goals through small steps
3. Create new success routines using the Three R's (Reminder, Routine, & Reward)
4. Use gratitude to celebrate the abundance in your life
5. Believe it is possible, then you will see it is

SUMMARY

Belief in your skills, experience, and intellect can be the determining factor between success and falling short. Belief in your ability to adapt and persevere in the face of challenge will keep you growing as your competition is left behind. Belief is your secret sauce that unleashes and amplifies all that makes you special. No salesperson, leader, or speaker can fully serve others without belief in the value they bring. Foster lasting belief in yourself by first looking for new ways to grow each day in your career and personal life. Next, celebrate the abundance that is already in your life and all that is still to come through expressions of gratitude. Finally, take control of the story you tell yourself, keeping your focus on bringing your aspirations to life.

Let your belief in who you are and what you do drive you to succeed.

YOU ARE INVINCIBLE

"Today is your day! Your mountain is waiting. So...get on your way!"
— Dr. Seuss

When I was 7 years old, my Invincible belief was put to the test one day when my brother Matt pointed at a tall tree and said, "I bet you are too weak to climb that!" Well, I loved to climb, so I snapped, "I am not weak. I am Invincible!" and I raced up the tree. When I reached the top, I was looking way down at the roof of our two-story house. Of course, just then, my mom runs outside, horrified. "Mark Allen Steel!" (Yeah, I got all three names!) "You get down here right now!" To which I foolishly responded, "Don't you worry, Mom. I'm Invin—"

To this day, I still remember falling. With a loud crack, the branch I was standing on broke free. Suddenly, I am rushing at the ground. I screamed in terror, knowing I was about to die. I probably would have, if three-quarters of the way down, I had not caught a limb right in the middle of my stomach. All the air exploded out of my body before I rolled off the branch and landed on the ground in an unconscious clump. The good news–I had only broken my arm. The bad news–the cast came off before I was done being grounded for my foolish act. Even worse, that fall led me to make an unnerving new discovery: "I guess I am not Invincible."

I now see that the 7-year-old me was wrong. Not just wrong to listen to my 9-year-old brother when he goaded me up a tree. I was *definitely* wrong about that. The younger me was wrong to think I was not Invincible—because I am. **We all are.** Of course, physically, none of us are Invincible. Each time I hear my body creak, crackle, or pop when I move, I am reminded my body is not Invincible. Yet the spirit within us is Invincible. **Any day, *every* day, you can choose to be Invincible.** You can choose to keep growing, learning, and moving forward. You can choose not to be defeated by setbacks and obstacles. You can choose to leave commonality, complacency, and clumsiness to your competitors and detractors. You can choose to accomplish all you set out to accomplish. In fact, you can demand it!

Each of you, as salespeople, leaders, and speakers, are here to serve. You have a chance to improve the lives and livelihood of others. The opportunity you have is to discover how best to serve others and then go out and do just that with resolute purpose. Use the 6 Invincible Principles to guide you. First, create intentional connection with your customer through your ability to ask great questions and listen with the intent to learn. Next, build trust through demonstrations of your ability, consistency, integrity, and responsibility. Doing these two helps you define a bold vision for your customer, anchored with value and supported by an incredible team. This is the foundation needed to speak with impact every time you communicate with others, delivering a message that engages and moves them to act. Use great stories that ensure you sell with confidence and lead with purpose. Finally, foster lasting belief in your skills and tenacity through growth, gratitude, and the story you tell yourself.

If you use these principles to guide your customer interactions, you will fundamentally shift your relationship with those you serve. I am walking, talking proof that they work. I was a guy with no college degree or sales background and I was on track to be fired after one year on the job. I learned not only to survive but also to thrive. You will, too!

When you combine your unique offering with relentless determination and a proven process to achieve results, you are Invincible!

You are Invincible salespeople, leaders, and speakers. You are here to live an Invincible life! You are here to do something special. You have an opportunity to serve others in a way that is unique to you. You are here to lead, not to follow. You will fundamentally change your relationship with those you serve by becoming a strategic partner in their success. You will achieve exceptional results.

Just remember, every now and then, as you did when you were a kid – grab the nearest towel, wrap it around you like a cape, stand up tall, and declare to the world,

"I AM INVINCIBLE!"

Did you find
Invincible Success
beneficial?

Additional content, including how to share this program with your team or organization, can be found by visiting:

https://marksteel.com

Check it out today.

ABOUT THE AUTHOR

Mark Steel is an international keynote and TEDx speaker, sales consultant, podcast host, and the founder of Peak Potential Solutions, LLC.

In his 14 years with Microsoft, Mark stood out as a high-impact sales leader with over $1B in sales. He has worked with many of the world's leading organizations, including McDonald's, Abbott, United, Allstate, State Farm, Caterpillar, Northwestern Mutual, and many more. Additionally, he has led regional training programs for hundreds of highly skilled sales experts.

Today, Mark speaks to audiences and organizations around the world. Through his engaging programs, podcast, and YouTube channel, Mark inspires professionals to sell with confidence, lead with purpose, and speak with impact.

Mark is a member of the National Speakers Association and Windy City Professional Speakers. He is an active member of Toastmasters, where he routinely delivers his programs to promote club and member growth.

His *Invincible Success* podcast, which helps you amplify your sales, leadership, speaking, and life, can be found on your favorite podcasting platforms. His TEDx speech can be viewed from his website. Also look for Mark on YouTube, plus other live-streaming and social media platforms.

Mark is a married father of two and resides in Woodridge, IL. He enjoys rock climbing, running, hiking, and reading.

Mark's Website: https://marksteel.com

Connect with Mark on Social Media:

- LinkedIn: linkedin.com/in/steelspeaking
- Facebook: facebook.com/steelspeaking
- Twitter: @steelspeaking
- Instagram: @steelspeaking

IN GRATITUDE

I am grateful for my beautiful wife, Jodi.
I am grateful for my two amazing kids, Jace and Cassidy.
I am grateful for my loving mother, father, my two great brothers, my best friend, my super cool pup, and all the other family and friends who love and support me.
I am grateful for my health and all that it allows me to do.

I am grateful for all the abundance in my life.

I am grateful for the abundance of success I already have and all the opportunity still to come.

I am grateful for the abundance of resources available to me, for the peers and mentors from whom I learn, and for the community that supports and encourages me.

I am grateful for the abundance of drive, tenacity, and willingness to work hard.

I am grateful for the abundance of Invincible Spirit within me.

REVIEWS

"From the very beginning, it is clear that *Invincible Success* is written by someone with years of firsthand experience in increasing sales and delighting customers. Mark's writing and speaking experience is evident through **a brilliant blend of storytelling, useful insights, and a continuous focus on helping others succeed.** All of us can overcome our own doubts to build a rewarding and prosperous career. *Invincible Success* shows us exactly how it's done. Well done!"

— Curt Mercadante, Founder - Merc Enterprises, LLC and best-selling author of *Five Pillars of the Freedom Lifestyle*

"Filled with inspiring stories, personal anecdotes, and life lessons, Mark Steel's book, *Invincible Success*, lays out the path to becoming extraordinary, not only at sales, speaking, and leadership, but at life itself. Weaving personal experiences and anecdotes with powerful, doable, and practical advice, Mark provides the perfect antidote to the "mind-clutter" that can prevent us from becoming the best. **If you want to achieve the seemingly impossible, you must read *Invincible Success*!"**

— Vincent C Racioppo, Ph.D., President - Center for Expert Performance, Inc.

"***Invincible Success* is a must read.** If you follow the principles in this book you will get results. Mark has made this an easy read with some really great stories. This book is both informative and inspirational. I highly recommend *Invincible Success*. It is **a 'Must Have' toolkit for anyone in sales and leadership!"**

— Sherlaender "Lani" Phillips, Vice President of US Partner Sales - Microsoft

"If you want to fulfill your potential as a professional in sales, influence, and leadership then this is a must read book. Mark shares timeless advice with modern day applications that will help you break through your personal barriers and achieve new levels of success. **This is a powerful tool that I wish I would have had years ago."**
— Mareo McCracken, Chief Revenue Officer- Movemedical

"Imagine immediately improving your leadership, sales and speaking; it is possible with *Invincible Success***!**
Mark Steel is a very knowledgeable and surprisingly humble guy, especially considering his amazing accomplishments such as exceeding over $1 billion in sales at a Fortune 50 company and then building his own phenomenal speaking and sales consulting career. That expertise and caring comes through in this book.
Mark's personal stories and practical ideas **will be a game-changer for you!"**
— Sarah Victory, International Speaker and best-selling author of *How to be Powerful*

"*Invincible Success* is an inspiring guide on how to successfully get out there and win! If you are looking to be a leader in sales, *Invincible Success* is a brilliant collection of relationship development lessons, essential sales mechanics, and real-life stories from successful leaders in sales. If you are struggling with your sales, this book will provide you with what you need to get back on track. If you are working hard and doubting yourself during difficult times, **if you are looking to build your own business to stratospheric success, Mark's book is the place to start.** If you are going to learn sales from someone, no one better than from the person who had over a billion dollars in sales, Mark Steel."
— Barbara Wichman, Global speaker, Leadership Coach, and Acclaimed Author of *The Leadership Tinderbox*

"**This book is a must read for anyone who wants to positively impact and influence others.** Whether you are in sales, or in a leadership role, you can only be effective at influencing others if you first believe in yourself. **Mark Steel not only equips you with the bullet-proof, superhero confidence that you need, he then teaches you how to use that confidence to powerfully and effectively connect and inspire others** to better their lives and be INVINCIBLE too. Mark has been an influential keynote speaker for many years. I was not at all surprised by the uniqueness, yet practicality of his latest book *Invincible Success*. His chapter on Storytelling provides mastermind principles and practices that will have your audience on the edge of their seats. Speakers can avoid spending hours and money on this concept because Mark has provided the recipe for great storytelling which is essential for any effective and impactful presenter."
    — Michelle Calloway, CEO - REVEALiO, Inc., Founder - Tech With Heart Foundation

"I am impressed with the flow of the book, the ease of reading and the practical information and exercises provided. **This book is a must-have for everyone** regardless of your functional area or business. This the best book I have encountered that provides the necessary framework to capture, entertain and inspire your audience. I can't imagine someone stepping on a stage without having read this book.
We are Invincible!"
    — Tanjia M. Coleman, PhD

"**Full of essential techniques you can implement immediately!**
Great success is achieved while serving others is the message of *Invincible Success*. Mark Steel shares his practical lessons learned during his highly successful sales career in a step by step system to take readers to their own personal triumphs. Most importantly he gives us the "why" behind each of those critical steps to keep readers motivated to take action."
    — Debbie Vyskocil, President - Optimal Edge Performance

"**This is a fantastic read** that feels like getting advice from a friend. Mark takes the common sense of building great relationships and provides the tools, techniques and motivation to help every person in sales - from closer to CEO - and make it genuine and natural."
   — Jake Jordan, Founder - Impact Over Attention

"*Invincible Success* is both empowering and enjoyable to read. Mark taps into our childhood beliefs that all of us can be superheroes and carries that idea into adulthood in such a relatable manner that I immediately connected with the principles he shares. A blueprint for getting ahead, *Invincible Success* is different from other Sales or Mindset books I've read because it conjures emotion, inspires original ideas, and lays out an actionable step-by-step methodology for tapping into and leveraging our inner superhero: our 'gift' that the world NEEDS.

I am delighted to highly recommend this book. **It has instantly become part of our training program** at the organization I chair. Three cheers for *Invincible Success* and to the superhero in us all!"
   — Cory Warfield, Co-Founder and Chief Visionary Officer - Shedwool

"**This book is packed with action steps that anyone in sales, leadership, or speaking can put to use immediately.** Mark's storytelling makes this book compelling, clear, and inspiring. Do yourself a favor, get this book today. **Highly recommend!**"
   — Shay Rowbottom, CEO - Shay Rowbottom Marketing

www.ingramcontent.com/pod-product-compliance
Lightning Source LLC
Chambersburg PA
CBHW071456080526
44587CB00014B/2119